TRADE LIBERALISATION POLICIES IN MEXICO

ORGANISATION FOR ECONOMIC CO-OPERATION AND DEVELOPMENT

:CONOMIC CO-OPERATION
VELOPMENT

Pursuant to Article 1 of the Convention signed in Paris on 14th December 1960, and which came into force on 30th September 1961, the Organisation for Economic Co-operation and Development (OECD) shall promote policies designed:

- to achieve the highest sustainable economic growth and employment and a rising standard of living in Member countries, while maintaining financial stability, and thus to contribute to the development of the world economy;
- to contribute to sound economic expansion in Member as well as non-member countries in the process of economic development; and
- to contribute to the expansion of world trade on a multilateral, non-discriminatory basis in accordance with international obligations.

The original Member countries of the OECD are Austria, Belgium, Canada, Denmark, France, Germany, Greece, Iceland, Ireland, Italy, Luxembourg, the Netherlands, Norway, Portugal, Spain, Sweden, Switzerland, Turkey, the United Kingdom and the United States. The following countries became Members subsequently through accession at the dates indicated hereafter: Japan (28th April 1964), Finland (28th January 1969), Australia (7th June 1971), New Zealand (29th May 1973), Mexico (18th May 1994), the Czech Republic (21st December 1995) and Hungary (7th May 1996). The Commission of the European Communities takes part in the work of the OECD (Article 13 of the OECD Convention).

Publié en français sous le titre :

POLITIQUES DE LIBRE-ÉCHANGE AU MEXIQUE

FOREWORD

In line with past practice of reviewing trade policies of new OECD Members, the Trade Committee has undertaken an examination of Mexican trade policies. This study begins with an overview of the broader context of the Mexican trade policy setting, including a brief survey of past reforms and a discussion of the 1994 financial crisis. Mexico's trade and trade-related policies, including its commitments in regional trading agreeements and in the World Trade Organisation are examined in this study. Particular attention is given to the task and challenges facing Mexican trade policy-makers in maintaining an open trade policy in the face of contrary pressures for protection. This study is published on the responsibility of the Secretary-General of the OECD.

TABLE OF CONTENTS

ABBREVIATIONS

ACE	Economic Complementary Accord (Spanish abbreviation)
AMS	aggregate measure of support
APEC	Asia Pacific Economic Co-operation
CFC	Federal Competition Commission
CPI	consumer price index
EU	European Union
FEC	Federal Electricity Commission
FDI	foreign direct investment
FTA	Free Trade Agreement
G-3	Group of three (Mexico, Colombia, Venezuela)
GATS	General Agreement on Trade in Services
GATT	General Agreement on Tariffs and Trade
GDP	gross national product
HS	harmonised system
IPRs	intellectual property rights
LAIA	Latin American Integration Association (Spanish abbreviation)
LFCE	Federal Economic Competition Law
Mercosur	Common Market of the Southern Cone
MFA	Multifibre Arrangement
MFN	most-favoured nation
Nadbank	North American Development Bank
NAFTA	North American Free Trade Agreement
NICs	newly industrialised countries
NMX	voluntary quality standards (Spanish abbreviation)
NOM	mandatory technical standards (Spanish abbreviation)
PRIs	Revolutionary Institutional Party (Spanish abbreviation)
PSE	Pacto de Solidaridad Economica
SECOFI	Ministry for Trade and Industrial Development (Spanish abbreviation)
TRIMs	trade-related investment measures
TRIPs	trade-related intellectual property rights
UNCTAD	United Nations Conference on Trade and Development
WTO	World Trade Organisation

CHAPTER 1

INTRODUCTION

Mexico has undergone an economic transition in the last decade and a half that is extraordinary by any standards. In its pace, breadth and depth, Mexico's reform process has surpassed those of most other developing countries that have undergone similar economic adjustments in recent years. And in comparison to the gradual evolution into modern economies of today's industrial countries, the speed of change in countries like Mexico looks even more dramatic.

Before 1982, Mexico relied heavily on import-substitution policies, emphasizing industrialisation, infrastructure development and economic diversification. Fledgling industries were shielded from import competition, and the costs of this protection were born by established economic activities. The agricultural and oil sectors made significant contributions in this regard. Trade was carefully managed. The overvaluation of domestic currency allowed relatively cheap imports of essential industrial inputs, while less essential imports were physically rationed or excluded altogether. Exports played a limited role in economic diversification, as most new industries concentrated on supplying the domestic market. While these policies contributed to the establishment of an industrial base and the modernisation of the Mexican economy, their long-term success would inevitably be compromised by the limited size of the domestic market, and by inefficiency and a lack of competitiveness in some branches of economic activity.

By the time of the debt crisis in 1982, growth was already being hampered by the intrinsic limitations of the previous policies. The immediacy of the debt crisis softened resistance to change and launched what was to become a sustained and far-reaching programme of reform. On the trade policy front, significant change did not begin until 1985, and from then on tariffs tumbled, quantitative restrictions and import licensing began to disappear, and exports started to play a major role in the economy. Trade policy is, of course, only one part of the story. Many other policy changes were essential to progress towards fuller participation in the world economy. Macroeconomic stability was a *sine qua non* of stability and sustained growth. The importance of this factor cannot be over-emphasized, as the macroeconomic shock of early 1995 amply demonstrated.

Other key areas in which important changes were made include investment policy, privatisation, deregulation, competition policy, and institutional reform. A strongly nationalist view of foreign direct investment (FDI) prevailed until the early 1980s. Since then, the relevant laws and regulations have increasingly encouraged foreign investment, but always within the constitutional limits imposed on foreign ownership and control of certain national assets. A vigorous programme of privatisation was initiated after 1982, leading to the disappearance of nearly 800 parastatal companies during the 1982-88 period. Subsequently, many other large state-owned companies have been privatised. Deregulation and competition policy have gone hand-in-hand, creating new and equitable market opportunities in both the traded and non-traded sectors of the economy. Finally, institutional reform of various kinds has been a vital element of modernisation. This study refers briefly to the reform of the national customs administration as an illustration of what is involved and why it is important.

On the institutional side, Mexico's membership of the OECD is symbolic of the achievements of the last few years. Perhaps most influential of all from the perspective of policy formulation has been the membership of the North American Free Trade Agreement (NAFTA). The prerequisites of NAFTA membership were instrumental in defining the content and pace of several aspects of Mexico's reforms. Joining GATT in 1986, and participating actively in the Uruguay Round, have also contributed to policy formulation, and been important in defining Mexico's role and position in the world economy. Mexico continues to extend regional initiatives beyond NAFTA, to other parts of Latin America and to Asia and Europe. These efforts, together with an active involvement in the multilateral trading system, testify to the awareness of the authorities of the value of diversified economic relations, especially in the circumstance where North American economic links are so predominant.

This study is particularly concerned with two challenges facing Mexican economic policy makers. The first relates to trade policy, and the unrelenting task of maintaining open trade policies in the face of contrary pressures. The management of "contingency" trade policies such as anti-dumping, countervailing duties and safeguards is crucial in this respect, along with policies in the areas of standards, marking, labelling and rules of origin.

The decision to raise some tariffs following the economic crisis of early 1995 is an example of how pressure from domestic industries can build into trade restrictions. The second policy challenge is more about trade relations, and the issue of coherence among overlapping trade agreements and commitments. Since these agreements and commitments are not identical, the issue to consider is whether they fit together and can coexist in reasonable harmony, or whether they engender inconsistencies and distortions that carry economic costs. Both these themes underlie much of the discussion in the subsequent chapters of this study.

Chapter 2 contains an overview of the broader, macroeconomic context of Mexican trade policy. This chapter also provides the statistical background for the rest of the study, indicating in particular the pattern and trends of trade and investment flows. Chapter 3 contains several short sections dealing with discrete elements of policy, some of which directly affect trade and others of which are only indirectly related, but which are nevertheless important for the overall coherence of open trade policies. Sections included in this chapter cover Mexico's multilateral trade policy, contingency trade policy, technical standards, marking, labelling and non-preferential rules of origin, deregulation, trade facilitation and sectoral policy, institutional reform in customs, privatisation and competition policy, and investment policy. Chapter 4 contains an analysis of NAFTA and other regional trade agreements. Chapter 5 examines the results of the Uruguay Round and Mexico's participation in the negotiations. Finally, Chapter 6 contains the summary and conclusions of the study, focusing especially on the two issues raised in the previous paragraph.

CHAPTER 2

THE ECONOMIC CONTEXT

1.   A brief history of reform

In December of 1994 Mexico entered its second major financial crisis in as many decades, requiring painful economic adjustment similar to that experienced after 1982. As in the previous crisis, a large current account deficit and capital outflows forced the Central Bank to retire from foreign exchange markets and allow the currency to devalue. Also as in the previous crisis, the trade balance turned around remarkably quickly, moving from a deficit of US$8.8 billion in the first six months of 1994 to a surplus of US$3.8 billion for the same period in 1995. The change in the trade balance is encouraging, but important challenges lie ahead. The most urgent problem is to contain the high inflation unleashed by such an abrupt adjustment of the exchange rate and to restore growth of per capita income. The difficulties in returning to a stable growth path are not negligible, but there is reason for some optimism given the comprehensive reforms that were undertaken in the economy over the past eight years. This chapter reviews these reforms beginning with trade policy and complementary policies for the liberalisation of the domestic market. The principal elements of macroeconomic reform and stabilisation are then outlined and a brief account is made of the recent financial crisis and its implications for trade policy. This is followed by a review of recent developments in the structure of trade, bilateral trade flows and FDI. This material is presented as a backdrop for more detailed coverage of trade and trade-related policies in the body of the report.

2.   Trade reform

Before the debt crisis of 1982 Mexico was a substantially closed economy, the legacy of 30 years of inward-oriented growth and an oil boom which had allowed policy makers to postpone economic reform. During the years of import-substitution, balance-of-payments crisis had traditionally led to a tightening of import restrictions as a way to economise on scarce foreign exchange. The debt crisis of 1982 was no different: 60 per cent of the value of all imports in 1979 was subject to licensing requirements; by December of 1982 this was extended to 100 per cent. It was not until 1984 that a consensus was reached within the government that trade restrictions were inimical to further growth. In December of that year the first fledgling signs of opening in the trade regime began with the elimination of licensing requirements for 17 per cent of all imports (Table 1).

Two events hastened the liberalisation between 1985 and 1987. The first was the decision to join the General Agreement on Tariffs and Trade (GATT), for which Mexico entered into negotiations in November of 1985 and was accepted in June of 1986. As part of this commitment, Mexico reduced import licenses to cover only 27.8 per cent of the value of imports. In addition, the trade weighted average tariff was reduced to 13.1 per cent and the dispersion was reduced.

Second, trade policy became an integral part of economic stabilisation when a number of external economic shocks in 1986 and 1987 led to the threat of hyperinflation[1]. Year on year inflation in 1987 was 160 per cent, the highest Mexico had experienced since the Revolution of 1910. To halt the increase in prices, the government designed a stabilisation package which added a strong component of incomes policy to traditional monetary and fiscal policies. Accelerated trade liberalisation was a key component of this programme, based on the assumption that competition from imports would put a ceiling on inflation for traded goods. By 1989 the trade weighted average tariff was brought down to 9.7 per cent and dispersion was reduced to 5 different levels, with a maximum of 20 per cent. In addition, licenses were reduced from 1 200 tariff lines to 325, although those remaining still accounted for about 20 per cent of the value of all imports[2]. All official import reference prices were eliminated.

The pursuit of a free trade agreement with the United States was a natural complement to these initiatives, and was announced in the middle of 1990, negotiated during 1991 (when Canada joined the negotiations) and 1992, and signed in December of that year. NAFTA was passed by the respective legislative bodies of the three countries in 1993 and went into effect in January of 1994[3]. NAFTA formed a cornerstone of the Mexican government's economic policy for a number of reasons. It was symbolic of the government's belief that future growth of the Mexican economy depended on access to foreign markets and foreign investment. The United States was the closest and most natural export market for Mexico and its major source of foreign capital. The pursuit of deeper trade and investment relations with the United States was an about-face in foreign commercial policy for Mexico, since its efforts in this area had traditionally been to diversify its economic relations away from the United States.

NAFTA was also a natural extension of trade liberalisation. The Agreement put in place a process of gradual liberalisation of the trade regime that will do away with most tariffs and quantitative restrictions on trade with Canada and the United States by the year 2004[4]. Since the majority of Mexican trade (86 per cent of exports and 73 per cent of imports of commodities in 1993, and growing in 1994)[5] takes place with NAFTA countries, this is tantamount to liberalisation of a very large portion of trade over the next ten years[6]. In addition, NAFTA instituted changes in the regulatory regime that were designed to make Mexico more attractive to both foreign and domestic private investors. These policy changes, discussed in more depth below, included the creation of a strong regime for intellectual property rights and a liberal environment for FDI.

Finally, NAFTA provided a template for Mexico's efforts to liberalise trade with other countries in the hemisphere. After the passage of NAFTA Mexico continued to seek free trade agreements with other countries in Latin America, and concluded such agreements with Bolivia, the other members of the G-3 (Colombia and Venezuela), Costa Rica, and is currently negotiating agreements with other countries in Central America, Ecuador and the members of the Common market of the Southern Cone (Mercosur)[7]. In most of these agreements, the NAFTA framework was used as a basis for negotiation, and was adopted with specific changes related to the negotiating requirements of each country.

3.   Complementary reforms for domestic market liberalisation

The elimination of restrictions on trade and FDI was the first step the government took to open up domestic markets for goods and services to effective competition. Privatisation was a complementary policy that broadened the scope for private sector participation in the economy and set schedules for the elimination of monopoly and oligopoly privileges in several sectors (communications and banking, for example). In addition, deregulation in a number of crucial areas was designed to facilitate private sector investment and remove the dead-weight loss and rent-seeking behaviour. However, opening up to foreign markets does not guarantee the benefits of competition without some effective deterrent to anti-competitive behaviour. To safeguard competition the government created the Federal Competition Commission in 1993. The Commission is charged with investigating and making determinations on the effects of market sharing and price-fixing behaviour of firms and evaluating mergers for their effects on the structure of markets. This initiative was considered a necessary step to increasing the contestability of local markets for domestic and foreign investors alike.

These complementary policy initiatives will be discussed more thoroughly in the next chapter of the study. They are mentioned here to signal that trade reform was not an isolated policy, but rather a part of a comprehensive package of microeconomic reforms designed to facilitate economic restructuring. A necessary condition for the success of such policies was macroeconomic stabilisation, an issue to which is going to be considered below.

4. Macroeconomic stabilisation and growth

As for most of Latin America, Mexico spent the better part of the 1980s engaged in the task of macroeconomic stabilisation. During the first part of the decade, authorities followed traditional stabilisation policy: a reduction in the government budget deficit, a tight monetary policy to curb inflation and an undervalued currency to restore balance-of-payments stability. This approach was only partially successful, overachieving its targets in the balance-of-payments, but failing to reduce inflation or return the country to previous levels of economic growth. Part of the problem was the link between the exchange rate and the internal price level. Devaluation was necessary to deal with the tight external and savings constraints imposed on Mexico by the debt crisis, but it also resulted inexorably in upward pressure on the price level. The tight savings constraints also made it impossible for the economy to resume growth without considerable inflation. By 1984-85, policy makers in Mexico had gauged the magnitude of the crisis and determined that in addition to standard macroeconomic measures a comprehensive microeconomic reform was necessary to change the orientation of the economy towards export growth. The reforms in trade barriers mentioned above were one of the first steps in this direction. By the beginning of 1985, two years after the debt crisis inflation still remained high, economic growth was slow, but the current account balance was in surplus and some structural reforms were beginning to be implemented.

In 1985 and 1986 Mexico was hit by two external shocks that severely complicated the task of macroeconomic stabilisation. The most important of these was the further decline in the international price of petroleum from

US$25.35 per barrel in 1985 to US$11.88 per barrel in 1986. Additionally, an earthquake hit Mexico City in September 1985. These shocks induced a further depreciation of the real exchange rate that contributed to an increase in the inflation rate. In 1985 inflation reached 63.7 per cent and increased in 1986 to slightly over 100 per cent (Chart 1).

Inflation was further aggravated by the speculative attack on the peso that occurred in 1987. High inflation during the year caused a drastic decline in real interest rates and a flow of financial resources into secondary markets -- in particular the Mexican Stock Market. This rapid growth of investment in the stock market came to a sudden halt in October 1987 with the crash in the New York Stock Exchange. Faced with a sudden decline in the price of stocks, investors moved into dollar denominated assets. In addition, based on the programme for debt reduction instituted by the government, the private sector received new lines of credit which, instead of being used for investment, were used to prepay a large portion of their foreign debt at a discount. The monetary authorities perceived this as a sign of a possible speculative attack on the peso and withdrew from the currency markets to protect the level of reserves. This resulted in a speculative attack on the currency and a large devaluation with consequent increases in the rate of inflation. Annualised quarterly inflation in the last part of 1987 reached as high as 225 per cent (Chart 2).

These circumstances led to a revision of macroeconomic stabilisation policy. Faced with evidence that orthodox stabilisation was not sufficient, since the reduction of the government deficit and economic growth had little effect on inflation, the government decided to add a strong component of incomes policy to these more traditional measures. The introduction of this "heterodox" approach recognised that there were structural characteristics in the economy that perpetuated inflation independently of the level of aggregate demand. These included the implicit and explicit indexation of wages to the price level, the high level of protection of the economy that did not allow effective competition from imports, and the high component of imported inputs that made the price level very sensitive to devaluation of the currency. In this highly inflationary environment, different sectors of the economy protected their income by continuing to increase prices. The incomes policy component aimed at arresting this inertial inflation by distributing the costs of disinflation among the major actors in the economy in an explicit and coordinated fashion. In Mexico this mechanism was instituted under what was known as the Pactos, the first of which was the *Pacto de Solidaridad Económica* (PSE) or simply the *Pactos*.

The *Pactos* drew on the experience of other countries such as Brazil, Argentina and Israel, which had shown that the implementation of incomes policies was a necessary, although not sufficient, condition to halt inflation. To these policies the *Pactos* added a significant fiscal adjustment: a correction of public sector prices, privatisation of publicly owned enterprises, and a reduction of current government expenditures. In addition, at the end of 1986 the government undertook a comprehensive fiscal reform that lowered the marginal tax, but increased the tax base and collections efficiency, resulting in an increase in government revenue. While a dramatic reduction in government expenditure (mostly at the cost of public investment) had brought the primary fiscal deficit (financial deficit less interest payments) into surplus since 1983, it was not until after the Pactos that public finances moved entirely into surplus, and the government became a net creditor to the private sector (Chart 3).

The centrepiece of the *Pactos* was a mechanism of consultation through which representatives of the main sectors of the economy (rural-farmers, the private sector, the government and organised labour) agreed upon the implementation of price controls and other measures that would eventually allow for a monthly rate of inflation of 2 per cent and a public sector primary surplus of 5 per cent per year. To let relative prices reach an equilibrium, the *Pactos* allowed for two months of price flexibility before price controls were imposed. During these two months (December 1987 and January 1988) accumulated inflation was 25 per cent (an accumulated annual rate of over 200 per cent). Subsequently, the *Pactos* fixed only the principal prices in the economy: the exchange rate, the prices of public sector services, wages, and the prices of a basket of "basic" goods to soften the effect of declines in real wages. The consensus nature of the *Pactos* allowed for a periodic revision of the goals and policies during the process of adjustment, making the mechanism flexible enough to incorporate new policy problems as they occurred[8].

The *Pactos* was a success in bringing down inflation in a short time with moderate cost in lost output. Annualised quarterly inflation fell from close to 200 per cent at the beginning of 1988 to below 20 per cent by the last quarter of the year (Chart 2) while the rate of growth of the gross domestic product (GDP), though low at 1.4 per cent, was not negative (Chart 4). In the wake of this success, the Salinas administration (1988-1994) decided that to reactivate economic growth it was necessary to reverse the net external resource transfers that had been occurring since 1982. The debt crisis had forced the economy to undertake an extraordinary savings effort, which was transferred abroad at an average rate of 6 per cent of GDP per year between 1983 and 1988[9]. The initiative to reverse this net transfer was the restructuring of government debt obligations to foreign creditors under the Brady Plan, which was expected to reduce debt payments by up to US$4.07 billion a year between 1990 and 1994[10]. Furthermore, in an effort to send a strong message to the private sector about the importance the government placed on private investment and repatriated capital in the growth programme, a sweeping initiative of privatisation was instituted, starting with the privatisation of the giant telephone monopoly (TELMEX) and continuing with the reprivatisation of the banking system among other important public enterprises[11]. In addition to these efforts, the conditions for private sector investment were improved through liberalisation of FDI provisions, extensive deregulation and a comprehensive reform of the financial system.

The solution to the debt problem developed in the Brady Plan and the subsequent negotiations with external creditors led the way for the return of Mexico to international financial markets. In addition, the positive expectations that developed as a result of the government's reform programmes led to large inflows of foreign capital. From 1991 to 1993 the capital account registered an average inflow of US$27.3 billion per year (Chart 5). This inflow relieved the savings constraint that Mexico had been experiencing since the early 1980s, allowing nominal interest rates to fall from an average of 50 to 10 per cent (Chart 6). This allowed private firms to begin to replace the capital stock that had depreciated considerably since the early 1980s, and reactivated economic growth. In 1990 GDP grew at 4.4 per cent, the fastest rate of growth since 1981.

However, large inflows of capital were also a mixed blessing. In addition to reversing the negative external resource transfers of the early 1980s, a major policy goal for the Salinas administration was the reduction of inflation to 5 per cent or lower, consistent with Mexico's major trading partners (principally the United States). During the first year of the *Pactos*, a reduction in inflation was achieved by fixing the exchange rate, effectively establishing price ceilings for traded goods at the level of the price of imports. After the first year, the exchange rate was allowed to fluctuate within a widening band, with a fixed floor at 3.0152 new pesos per US dollar and a ceiling that was allowed to increase at 0.0002 new pesos per day. This daily rate of depreciation was increased to 0.0004 new pesos in October of 1992.

Controlling the depreciation of the exchange rates neutralised inflation in the traded goods sector, but did not attack the problem for non-traded goods. The higher level of protection for non-traded goods and the relative lack of efficiency gains in this sector led to higher increases in prices here than in the economy overall. An examination of the consumer price index (CPI) for all goods versus for services (Chart 7) shows clearly how the price of services rose considerably faster than the overall price level. This was a direct effect of the large capital inflows, which are well known to cause an appreciation in the real exchange rate, evidenced by a change in the relative prices of traded versus non-traded goods. Hence capital inflows worked against the government's anti-inflation goal, making it more difficult to bring price increases down to single digit levels.

A concomitant effect of large capital inflows and the appreciation of the real exchange rate was a growing deficit in the current account. From a surplus of about 1.5 per cent of GDP in 1987 the current account moved towards a progressively greater deficit, reaching 2 per cent GDP in 1990, 3.6 per cent in 1991 and over 7 per cent in 1992 (Chart 8). In an attempt to reduce the growing trade deficit and quell inflation once and for all the government raised interest rates at the end of 1992 and 1993, bringing economic growth to a standstill (0.43 per cent in 1993) but reducing the current account deficit to 5.4 per cent of GDP and inflation from 12 per cent in 1992 to 8 per cent in 1993.

5.   The financial crisis of 1994-1995

At the beginning of 1994 the Salinas administration had some significant macroeconomic successes to its credit, including single digit inflation, an overall public sector surplus since the middle of 1980s, (meaning that rather than draining domestic savings, the government was a net creditor to the private sector), comprehensive economic reforms and the signing and passage of the NAFTA. These achievements created positive expectations for economic growth and seemed to guarantee a sizeable yearly flow of foreign capital to fund the large current account deficits the country was running. To support this position, in February of 1994 the Central Bank had the highest level of reserves in Mexico's history, at around US$29 billion. In short, the economy seemed to be poised for sustained economic growth with low inflation, that would lead to increases in per capita income that had been repeatedly unobtainable during the previous decade.

The large current account deficit was a natural effect of the excess of investment over savings that resulted from the large capital inflows throughout the period. The Salinas administration argued that the current account deficit was a natural condition for a developing country that required imports of capital goods to restructure its manufacturing sector. However, not all the capital inflows were being used to finance investments. The fastest growing component of imports from 1987 to 1994 was consumer goods, which grew at twice the rate of overall imports (Table 5)[12], although admittedly from a very low base. Nevertheless, imports of consumer goods never exceeded 12.5 per cent of total imports. The largest component of merchandise imports throughout the period were intermediate goods, which were necessary to support the impressive export performance of the Mexican economy.

More worrisome still was the fact that a large part of the current account deficit was financed by volatile short term capital flows. Chart 5 shows the composition of liabilities with the rest of the world in the capital account. The large inflows of capital beginning in 1990 are clearly visible, as well as the change in composition of these flows towards portfolio investments. From virtually no portfolio investment in 1987 and 1988, these flows came to make up 64 and 48 per cent of all foreign investment in 1992 and 1993 respectively, and 42 per cent in the first three quarters of 1994.

Moreover, the government's policy to contest inflation with its exchange rate commitment stifled economic growth and led to low levels of employment creation in the formal sector of the economy. Critics of the government's policy argued that the reactivation of economic growth required a real depreciation of the currency. This would switch demand from imports towards domestic goods and create the conditions necessary for a reactivation of economic growth. This measure would also reduce the trade deficit and make the country less dependent on volatile foreign capital. A depreciation of the currency could most effectively be achieved by a devaluation of the exchange rate, through a once-and-for-all shift in the band within which the exchange rate could fluctuate or an increase in the daily rate of depreciation.

The decision to devalue involved an economic trade-off for the governments' goals of economic stability and growth. On the one hand, maintaining the exchange rate regime ensured the reduction of inflation but risked poorer short term performance in.output and exports. On this point the government argued that the structural changes in both the private and the public sectors had set the base for rapid increases in productivity that would eventually lead to increases in exports growth and employment. This tendency was reinforced by the increases in domestic and foreign direct investment that had taken place over the last few years, and the new opportunities secured for exports by NAFTA and other trade agreements.

Furthermore, there was a danger that a large devaluation might make financial markets nervous and result in a crisis of confidence in the Mexican financial system. At the very least, a devaluation would cause an increase in inflation that might reverse the hard won gains of the past few years.

Faced with the choice, the government kept unaltered the exchange rate regime, convinced that the stability and predictability of the exchange rate was one of the most important assets it had in maintaining the credibility of its economic policies. An increase in capital inflows as a result of the substantial economic reforms undertaken by the Salinas administration was expected to lead to a natural appreciation of the real exchange rate, as expectations for economic growth and international competitiveness of the economy improved. Under this view, the daily mini-devaluations of the peso against the US dollar under the *Pactos* were sufficient to counteract the effects of inflation and keep the exchange rate in line with its real value. Nevertheless, there was some concern that if structural change in the external sector of the Mexican economy did not progress at the expected pace, the exchange rate regime could lead to an unsustainable situation. First, despite a 14 per cent depreciation of the peso within its flotation band during 1994, the accumulated real appreciation of the peso over the 1987-1994 period was significant. Chart 10 shows indices of real exchange rate comparing the Mexican consumer price index (in US dollar terms) with the US wholesale price index for different types of commodities. It remains that it is difficult to evaluate in the absolute whether costs and prices in Mexico in 1994 were already higher than in its main trade partners. Furthermore, as noted above, there were genuine reasons to believe that the significant adjustment of the recent period had significantly improved the export potential of the economy. Secondly, the growth in imports required to modernise the economy and to boost the export sector was still above the impressive growth in exports. From 1987 to 1994, exports grew at an average annual rate of 11.9 per cent, while imports grew at 22.8 per cent (Chart 9 -- Tables 2 and 5)[13]. It was the authorities view that with improved competitiveness resulting from the opening of the economy, the growth in exports would exceed in due time that of imports.

Thus, although Mexico entered 1994 with a much improved economic situation, it was still vulnerable to external shocks, particularly reversals in capital flows. This vulnerability was exacerbated by the well-known political events that rocked the country during 1994. In January, an armed uprising in the southern state of Chiapas staged by a group calling itself the Zapatista National Liberation Army (EZLN) demanded the removal of the government and radical changes in the political system. In March, the presidential candidate of the Revolutionary Institutional Party (PRI), well known for his reformist programme, was assassinated while campaigning in the north of the country. In July, the Secretary of the Interior resigned from his post alleging obstruction of the process of electoral reform[14]. In September, the director of the PRI, José Francisco Ruiz Massieu, also a reformer, was assassinated in Mexico City. In October, his brother, named deputy attorney general and special prosecutor in the investigation of the assassinations, also resigned alleging that there was obstruction in the investigations. Each one of these events had repercussions on the level of confidence perceived by external investors in Mexico.

The result of this increasing uncertainty and expectations for devaluation was a large reduction in capital inflows. Net capital inflows fell from US$10.7 billion in the first quarter of 1994 to US$7.39 billion in the second quarter and US$3.4 billion in the third. In contrast the liabilities incurred due to the deficit in the current account continued to grow. By the third quarter of 1994 Mexico had a current account deficit of US$22 billion with inflows of capital amounting to US$14.3 billion: the shortfall of US$7.7 billion had to be financed from reserves.

News of a worsening situation in Chiapas, shortly after the new government took office, fuelled uncertainty in December, bringing the level of reserves down to US$11 billion by the middle of the month. On 20 December, after consultations under the Pactos, the band within which the peso was allowed to float was widened (a *de facto* devaluation of 15 per cent). However, the market reaction was particularly severe reflecting a combination of factors. The devaluation represented the abandonment of a long-standing commitment which had been a centre-piece of the previous administration's policy strategy, and the delay before a convincing policy strategy could be put in place exacerbated the climate of uncertainty. In this environment, markets quickly came to the view that the 15 per cent devaluation was too small. After a further US$5 billion in reserves were lost in defending the new floor, the exchange rate was allowed to float freely on 22 December. The exchange rate fell below 6 pesos to the US dollar by the end of December (Chart 12)[15].

The peso's depreciation had immediate implications for all parts of the economy and led to a reassessment of the repayment capacity of both public and private Mexican debtors. The two main sources of concern were the fragility of the banking sector, which quickly appeared to reach a critical point, and the government's capacity to repay dollar-indexed securities (Tesobonos). In this climate, the stabilisation plan of 4 January 1995, that included fiscal stringency and strict wage guidelines as well as a tight monetary policy framework, failed to reassure markets. A financial support package engineered by the US Treasury, the International Monetary Fund, and other multilateral financial institutions was announced in mid-January 1995. However, it was not sufficient to restore confidence to financial markets and the peso continued to fall. The resulting instability in financial markets put additional pressures on the already fragile financial sector.

Despite a record of policy achievement over the previous dozen years, it has been difficult to restore a certain degree of confidence. Although the recovery of confidence is still incipient, it is a significant fact that less than six months after the December 1994 crisis, Mexican public and private sector entities had regained access to international capital markets. A key factor in beginning to rebuild financial confidence was the strengthening, in March 1995, of the Mexican government's stabilisation programme, buttressed by the announcement of an enhanced package of international liquidity support by President Clinton.

The government's stabilisation programme signifies a move to flexible exchange rates and the use of the money supply as an anchor for inflation. As long as prudent macroeconomic policies are maintained, the programme should be successful, inflation could fall considerably and growth could resume in 1996. For the first half of 1995, GDP was estimated to have fallen by 5.8 per cent in real terms compared with the first half of 1994. January to August 1995 inflation stood at 37.9 per cent, at this rate, it is likely that by year's end inflation will stand around 50 per cent. On a brighter note, as mentioned above, the trade balance has improved considerably for the first six months of 1995, with exports of US$38.3 billion and imports of US$35.2 billion yielding a net surplus of US$3.1 billion[16]. Bilateral trade with the United States, Mexico's principal trading partner, yielded a surplus of US$3.8 billion for the first quarter of 1995 compared to a deficit of US$534 million for the same period in 1994[17]. Foreign investment continues to enter the country, though not at the pace of previous years. Portfolio investment fell from US$3.4 billion in the first quarter of 1994 to a mere US$128 million in the corresponding quarter of 1995, but direct investments amounted to US$2.8 billion, many of which are in the maquiladora industry. International reserves held by the Central Bank were back up to US$15 billion at the end of August[18].

In addition to its stabilisation package, the Zedillo administration has implemented policies specifically related to trade. In this respect, the financial crisis presented the danger of providing an incentive for increased protectionism as a reaction to foreign exchange constraints, although the close to 50 per cent depreciation already provides an ample margin of protection across the board[19]. Notwithstanding, the Zedillo administration has maintained its liberal stance towards trade, and the surplus in the trade balance in 1995 seems to mitigate the pressure for higher protection. The administration confirmed its commitment to the free trade agreements (FTA) already signed, and has even entered into talks with Representatives of the European Union, Ecuador and Mercosur aimed at the eventual negotiation of a trade agreement. There has been an increase in tariffs from 20 to 35 per cent on clothing, shoes and manufactured leather imports from countries with which Mexico does not have a FTA. Although significant, this increase does not constitute much of a rise in protection since many of these products were already highly protected from the main sources of competition through anti-dumping and countervailing duties[20].

6.   The structure of trade

A.   *Merchandise exports*[21]

As can be seen in Chart 9, in the last years Mexico's exports have grown at an impressive pace, even though outperformed by imports. From 1987 to 1994 Mexican exports grew at an average annual rate of 11.9 per cent. It was not until recently that the growth rate of exports began to pick up, registering 12.3 per cent for 1993, and 17.2 per cent for 1994 (Table 2). This is an impressive rate of growth considering the overvaluation of the peso. More impressive still is the change in the composition of exports away from petroleum products and towards manufacturing. In 1987, petroleum products made up 31.2 per cent of total exports; in 1994 the figure was 12.1 per cent. The participation of manufacturing exports has increased from 61 to 80.9 per cent over the same period. The main component of this growth was in the maquiladora industry. While overall manufacturing exports grew at 16.3 per cent from 1987-1993, Maquiladora exports grew at 20.6 per cent.

Both within and outside the maquiladora industry, growth in exports has been mainly the result of investments in the automobile and auto parts industry and in electronic equipment manufacturing. Table 3 shows the structure of non-maquiladora manufactured exports. In 1982 the main manufactured exports were in the food processing sector (food, drink and tobacco), petroleum derivatives, chemicals, transportation equipment and other machinery and equipment. By 1993 the processed food, chemicals, and petroleum derivatives had lost importance, while transportation and machinery and equipment (mainly electronic equipment) had gained a predominant share. A similar trend has occurred in the maquiladora industry (Table 4), where by 1994 fully 78 per cent of exports were from the machinery and equipment sector (mainly electronic equipment), followed by 8 per cent in textiles.

B.   Merchandise imports

Mexico's merchandise imports grew at 22.8 per cent per year from 1987 to 1994. The fastest growing class was imports of consumer goods, which grew at 43.3 per cent per year (Table 5). This high rate may be somewhat misleading, since consumer goods imports started from a very low base in 1987, the year in which liberalisation of the trade regime began in earnest. Nevertheless, in terms of the structure of imports these types of goods increased their participation from 4 per cent in 1987 to 12 per cent in 1994. The bulk of imports continues to be intermediate goods, although their participation fell from 82 per cent in 1987 to 71.2 per cent in 1994. Capital goods imports grew on average by 26 per cent per year, increasing their participation from 14 per cent of all imports in 1987 to 16.7 per cent in 1994. Maquiladora imports, a component of intermediate imports, declined in importance from 29.3 per cent in 1987 to 25.8 per cent in 1994.

The structure of Mexican merchandise imports is similar to that of exports, a fact that stems from the large share of trade that is intra-firm and intra-industry, even outside the maquiladora. Intermediary goods have always predominated in Mexico's imports, but have become less important, declining from 81.9 per cent of all trade in 1987 to 71.2 per cent in 1994 (Table 5). Within manufacturing, automobiles and auto parts, and other machinery and equipment, have become slightly more important (Table 6). In the maquiladora industry, not surprisingly, the structure of imports matches that of exports, with a predominant share going to machinery and equipment, followed by plastics and rubber and textiles and apparel (Table 7).

C.   Trade balance

Mexico's merchandise trade balance moved into surplus after the 1982 debt crisis and remained in surplus until 1989, when large deficits began to reappear (Table 8). The main surplus sector is mining, principally composed of petroleum and natural gas, although this surplus has been declining in absolute terms since 1981. The main deficit sector is manufacturing, which increased considerably from 1989 to 1993. Within manufacturing, non-metallic and metallic minerals have consistently yielded slight surpluses while food, beverages and tobacco, textiles and apparel and transportation vehicle equipment have yielded pro-cyclical surpluses that moved into deficit in 1992 and 1993. Other manufacturing sectors with consistent large deficits were paper and printing, chemicals, and especially other machinery and equipment. In contrast, the maquiladora industry has consistently yielded a surplus, mainly due to the machinery and equipment exports (Table 9). Plastics and rubber and steel are large deficit items here.

D.   *Trade in services*

Mexico's trade in services (invisibles) has been consistently in deficit since 1985 mainly due to large interest payments on foreign debt, although insurance and freight payments have grown considerably, hand in hand with the growth of imports (Table 10). The principal surplus exports are tourism (inland tourism as opposed to border tourism) and transfers. Border tourism mostly represents the payments of Mexicans living on the US border to US border businesses -- a deficit which has declined considerably if not altogether disappeared after the devaluation of 1994. Transfers are made up principally of remittances of Mexican workers in the United States (i.e. exports of Mexican labour) which are a significant proportion (16 to 18 per cent) of total service exports. A large increase in repatriated profits and reinvested earnings reflect the increase in foreign direct investment in Mexico over the last five years.

E.   *Bilateral trade flows*

Mexico's principal trade partner continues to be the United States with 85 per cent of all exports and 69 per cent of imports in 1994 (Tables 11 and 12). Canada, by contrast, only received 2.4 per cent of exports and supplied 2 per cent of imports. The rest of Latin America received 6.9 per cent of all exports and supplied 4.7 per cent of all imports. The European Union (EU) has remained an important trading partner with 5 per cent of exports and 11 per cent of imports, as has Japan, with one per cent of exports and 5 per cent of imports. The growth of the maquiladora industry and liberalisation of trade between Mexico and its partners in North America have resulted in an increasing concentration of trade in this region.

The dramatic increase in Mexico's merchandise trade from 1987 to 1994 was also accompanied by a change in the structure of bilateral trade relations. Relations with most of the major trading partners moved into deficit along with the aggregate trade balance, but the composition of the balances has changed (Table 13). In 1992 the largest deficit was with the United States, followed by the EU and Japan. In 1993 and 1994 increased exports to the

United States reduced Mexico's bilateral trade deficit with this country, while increased imports led to a higher deficit with the EU and Japan. In Latin America, Brazil is a major deficit country while Mexico maintains a surplus with most other countries in this region.

The rapid adjustment of the balance of trade in 1995 changed the deficit with the United States into a surplus of US$6 billion. In addition, the large deficits with the EU, Japan and Asian newly industrialised countries (NICs) were considerably reduced.

7.   Foreign direct investment

FDI flows into Mexico have increased substantially over the 1980s, doubling the cumulative stock of foreign controlled fixed investments every 6 years (Table 14). Of particular note is the increase in investment in 1994, which almost doubled the previous yearly flows.

The sectoral distribution of FDI is concentrated in industry (manufacturing, construction and electricity generation), although the importance of this sector has diminished sharply in favour of services since 1986. The principal service sectors receiving FDI are (in order of importance): professional and technical services (35.6 per cent); real estate rental and administration (28.6 per cent); restaurants and hotels (16.8 per cent); finance and insurance (14 per cent); and other subsectors (4.9 per cent).

Not surprisingly, the main source of FDI has historically been the United States, although its share has been diminishing slightly (Table 15). In 1983, US investments made up 66 per cent of the accumulated investment in Mexico; in 1994 this figure had fallen to 61 per cent. Much of the decline was picked up by the United Kingdom, that increased its share from 3 per cent in 1983 to 7 per cent in 1993. Other countries, principally Spain, Holland, Sweden and Italy have also increased their share significantly.

NOTES

1   These included the earthquake that hit Mexico City in September 1985, the decline in the price of petroleum in 1986, and a run on the peso caused by the crash of the New York Stock Exchange in October 1987. The effects of these shocks are reviewed more completely below.

2   The majority of those items remaining under license requirements were in agriculture, petroleum, inputs into the capital goods and automobile industries, and a small portion of electronics, chemical and pharmaceutical goods.

3   Before NAFTA Mexico had already signed an agreement for economic co-operation with Chile that envisioned free trade. A description of the trade agreement and its implementation, as well as other regional arrangements, is given in Chapter 4.

4   In some cases the time period extends to 15 years. See Chapter 4.

5   See Tables 11 and 12 and the section on bilateral trade flows below.

6   Recent events after the crisis of December 1994 indicate that trade policy has shifted even more in favour of NAFTA countries by increasing the tariffs on selected imports from countries which do not have Free Trade Agreements (FTAs) with Mexico to highest levels allowable under the GATT (see below).

7   Mexico has sought to negotiate free trade agreements with the Mercosur countries (although these were suspended in 1994) and more recently with the European Union (in 1995).

8   For a description of successive versions of the *Pactos* see Rudiger Dornbusch and Alejandro Werner (1993), *Mexico, Stabilization, Reform, and No Growth*. Brooking Papers on Economic Activity, 1: 1994, pp. 253-315.

9   Lustig, Nora, Mexico, the Remaking of an Economy, The Brookings Institution, Washington D.C., 1992, Table 2-2, page 33.

10 Pedro Aspe Ormella, El camino mexicano de la transpomación economica, Fondo de Cultura Economico, Mexico D.F. 1994, pp. 126-127.

11 Privatisation was initiated by the de la Madrid administration but not on the scale of the Salinas administration's programme.

12 Admittedly, consumer imports grew from a very small base in 1987.

13 These figures include the maquiladora industry.

14 He subsequently took back his post and presided over what most observers agree were the cleanest elections in Mexico's history.

15 For a more detailed description of the financial crisis see OECD Economic Surveys, Mexico, September 1995.

16 The increase in exports was due in large part to agricultural products, particularly coffee beans, tomatoes, fruits, vegetables and live cattle. On the other hand, the decline in imports was principally due to consumer and capital goods, leaving intermediate goods imports largely unchanged. Exports from the maquiladora industry during the first two months of 1995 rose by 18.9 per cent over the same period the previous year.

17 US Department of Commerce figures show Mexican exports to the United States reached US$14.9 billion in the first quarter of 1995, up 32.2 per cent from the same period in 1994.

18 These figures speak to an improving macroeconomic situation, though certainly not one that will begin to produce substantial growth in per capita income or employment soon. An important question for 1995 is to what extent social unrest will develop as a result of increasing unemployment and the declines in real wages that follow from inflation.

19 Such a danger was realised in Brazil, for example, where tariffs on automobile imports have been increased to 150 per cent since January 1995.

20   In particular, this is true of imports of textiles from China. It is interesting to note, however, that some Mexican companies are becoming advocates of freer trade and challenging the government on this account. On 18 April 1995 a Mexican company (Ferreifel) obtained an injunction (amparo) against the Commerce Ministry (SECOFI) for slapping tariffs on its imports from China. The court ruled that only the President can issue tariff regulations, and the case will be heard in the Mexican Supreme Court. In the meantime, the company is exempt from paying import duties and the government must return moneys paid in the seven intervening months before the case was finally decided.

21   By convention the merchandise trade data presented in Mexico in the past has not included the maquiladora industry, since this was considered a component of services trade. In recent years this practice has changed and trade figures now include maquiladora imports and exports. Unless otherwise noted, all the aggregate figures presented here include maquiladora trade.

CHAPTER 3

THE TRADE AND TRADE-RELATED POLICY

FRAMEWORK

1.   Introduction

The process of trade liberalisation in Mexico has been accompanied by significant reforms in a number of other policy areas. Some of these reforms are discussed in the present chapter. In broad terms, two kinds of policies are considered here -- those that are natural accompaniments of trade liberalisation, and those that assume an importance they did not previously possess because any effects they may have exerted were largely swamped by the more pervasive influence of restrictive trade policies. In the first group, aspects of deregulation, trade facilitation, institutional reform in customs, privatisation, competition policy and investment policy are covered. Policies in all these areas have supported trade liberalisation and given the overall structure of economic policy a coherence it would otherwise lack.

In the second category, contingency trade policy (anti-dumping, countervailing duties, and safeguards) and technical standards, marking, labelling and non-preferential origin rules have been examined. As argued below, contingency trade policy, properly managed, has a crucial role to play as a safety valve, easing the costs of adjustment to foreign competition, and in some cases, providing a breathing space for firms to prepare for competition. If it is poorly managed, or relied upon in excess, contingency trade policy can arrest trade liberalisation and deny the economy the benefits of opening up to competition.

As far as standards, marking, labelling, and rules of origin are concerned, these are essential elements of modern trade policy. The maintenance of an adequate regime of standards, marking and labelling rules is a basic responsibility of government, but it is not difficult to see how these can be turned into instruments of surrogate protection. Similarly, non-preferential origin rules are necessary for the implementation of contingency trade policy measures and any other measures that require a clear identification of the origin

33

of goods, but these are also susceptible to manipulation in ways that can frustrate trade well beyond the intent of the underlying policies they are supposed to support.

An issue touched on briefly in this chapter is sectoral policy. It is taken up in the context of deregulation and trade facilitation. The reason for grouping sectoral policy with deregulation and trade facilitation in this discussion is that in its modern manifestation in Mexico, sectoral policy has much in common with these policies. Traditional sectoral policy tends to single out particular industries or even firms for special treatment, sometimes simply to protect them from competition, or at other times in the hope of targeting them for future success. By contrast, the basic thrust of Mexican sectoral policy is upon export competitiveness and the development of small and medium enterprises, where the creation of an enabling and more friendly environment for doing business constitutes the primary emphasis.

The chapter begins with a short account of the evolution of Mexico's trade policy in recent years, with particular reference to tariffs and non tariff measures. These issues are referred to further in Chapter 4 and Chapter 5, which deals respectively with Mexico's participation in NAFTA and in the Uruguay Round.

2.   Mexico's multilateral trade policy

Mexico has unilaterally liberalised its trade regime on a most-favoured-nation basis considerably since it entered the GATT in 1986, from a highly restrictive policy in which all imports were subject to licensing requirements, to a substantially open economy. Table 16 summarises the trade regime as it existed in December of 1993, with import figures for that same year. Import licensing restraints were reduced to cover only 1.6 per cent of all tariff lines, but these still made up 21.6 per cent of the value of imports. Most of these restraints applied to agricultural products, petroleum and petroleum products, and motor vehicles.

Imports on non-agricultural products are subject to *ad valorem* rates of duty varying from duty free to 20 per cent. These applied rates are much lower than corresponding levels at which Mexico has consolidated them against increases in the World Trade Organisation (WTO). In the context of the recent round of multilateral trade negotiations, the Uruguay Round, Mexico reduced the weighted average bound rate for all merchandise trade from 52.2 to 40.3 per cent. In December 1994, the simple average applied rate of duties on non-agricultural products was 12.5 or 11.3 per cent calculated on a weighted average basis (Table 18).

For agricultural products, non-tariff barriers, such as licenses and quantitative restrictions, were converted into tariff equivalents in 1994 to comply with Mexico's commitments under the Uruguay Round. As a result, *ad valorem* duties on agricultural products vary between 36 and 260 per cent. Agricultural imports only represented 2.6 per cent of total Mexican imports in 1993.

In addition to licensing, certain imports are prohibited. These include substances containing illegal drugs and used cars. There are also local content requirements in the motor vehicle industry. Mexico also applies a domestic value added tax regime at the rate of 15 per cent on most products and excise taxes on alcohol and cigarette products.

The policy towards exports has always been much more liberal than that for imports. Export taxes have been reduced along with tariffs, and the number of goods subject to export taxes and restraints has been reduced considerably. Most export licensing requirements are imposed on agricultural commodities, endangered species and petroleum derivatives. A duty drawback system has also been introduced for exports that have a high content of imported inputs.

In June 1995, the government announced tariff increases for manufactured leather articles (HS 4201 to 4304), apparel (HS 6101 to 6210) and footwear (HS 6401 to 6406) to 35 per cent from 20 per cent in most cases (15 per cent for a small fraction). These new rates are applied to cope with increasing imports affecting small and medium size enterprises in these sectors. Nevertheless these rates are still below the GATT bound rates and will be applied on a temporary basis.

3.   **Contingency trade policy**

Like most countries adopting a liberal trade regime, Mexico has introduced an anti-dumping and countervailing duty statute. Mexico has also established a safeguards mechanism, something that relatively few developing countries have done. The anti-dumping provisions allow domestic producers to petition the authorities when they consider that dumped imports are causing or threatening to cause material injury to a domestic industry. Dumping is defined as selling in an export market at a price below the prevailing price in the domestic market of the seller. Dumping is considered an unfair trade practice, and if a domestic producer petitions for anti-dumping duties, the law permits the competent authorities to apply anti-dumping duties, provided dumping and injury are found, and causality is established between the two. The rules on countervailing duty are very similar, the major difference being that the source of injury in this case is the use of subsidies by the government of the exporting country. The safeguard provisions permit the authorities to impose duties on imports if the domestic producers of the same or similar products are suffering serious injury as a result of the imports. The most important difference between safeguard actions and anti-dumping and countervailing duties is that safeguards are not justified in terms of unfair trade practices by foreign firms or governments. Instead, they reflect a decision by the government to provide a margin of protection to a domestic industry in the face of strong competition from imports.

A.   *Anti-dumping and countervailing duties*

Mexico's anti-dumping and countervailing duty system was formally established in 1986[1], at around the time Mexico joined the GATT. Legislation and regulations have been updated over time, including to accommodate evolving international rules and commitments under NAFTA and other regional agreements. The most significant legislative changes are those contained in the 1993 Foreign Trade Law, which sought to establish a comprehensive framework for international trade laws and regulations, to promote Mexico's international competitiveness, to ensure the efficient use of the nation's resources, and to guarantee legal security for enterprises engaged in international trade. The new law also attempted to address particular problems that had arisen in the 1986 legislation with respect to procedural aspects of anti-dumping and countervailing duty actions, including in relation to rights of representation, transparency, and time frames for investigations.

The new law has introduced procedural improvements in many areas. Among these are provisions for access to confidential information, public hearings concerning the facts of a case, requirements for petitions, standards of evidence, notification and verification procedures, and the duration of anti-dumping and countervailing duties. Rights of representation for interested parties in a case have been extended on equal terms to cover national producers, importers, foreign exporters, and other foreign interested parties, including governments as well as the Federal Competition Commission. As far as the time frame for investigations is concerned, the new law stipulates 130 working days for a preliminary finding, and a further 130 days for a final determination. These periods are the same as those used by the United States and Canada. Further modifications may be required in Mexico's anti-dumping and countervailing duty laws and/or regulations following the entry into force of the relevant WTO agreements on 1 January 1995. Examination in the WTO regarding the consistency of the Mexican law with WTO agreements is under way.

Despite being relatively frequent users of anti-dumping, Mexican Authorities have made serious efforts to infuse a certain amount of economic rationality into the system. Greater emphasis has been placed on economic considerations than in many other countries, where a more legalistic approach has tended to dominate. As a result of this approach, the Ministry for Trade and Industrial Development (Secretaría de Commercio y Fomento Industrial, or SECOFI) conceptualises the injury arising from dumped imports as the amount of price undercutting with respect to a national world price: the idea being that, in absence of the dumped imports, the domestic prices in the country of importation can only rise up to world prices and not the domestic prices in the country of exportation (the so-called "normal value"). The practical effect of this policy is to limit the anti-dumping duty to an amount less than the full margin of dumping. This is an improved version of the "lesser duty rule" since the applicable benchmark for assessing injury (the world price) is a known parameter. Of course, SECOFI can only use this scheme provided there is in fact a known world price and as long as this world price is relatively unaffected by distortions.

Between 1987 and March 1995, Mexico initiated 193 anti-dumping and countervailing investigations against 40 countries. Of these, 176 were anti-dumping cases, and the remaining 17 were in respect of subsidies. The United States accounted for by far the majority of these cases (51 cases), which can be explained by its large bilateral trade flows. Anti-dumping actions against China have been numerous (37 cases), and in some cases have led to very high anti-dumping duties. Other countries against which a significant number of cases have been brought include Brazil (22 cases), Germany (9 cases), Venezuela (8 cases), and Korea (7 cases). All these countries taken together account for about 70 per cent of all cases taken. Of the 193 cases brought, 126 of them, or about 65 per cent, have ended in definitive findings or actions of one kind or another. About 35 per cent (57 cases) of these have resulted in the imposition of definitive anti-dumping or countervailing duties. Of the as yet unresolved cases, twelve currently incur provisional anti-dumping duties. Between 1991 and early 1995, 43 petitions were rejected by SECOFI on the grounds of inadequate evidence either of the alleged unfair trade practice or of injury, or of a causal link between dumping/subsidisation and injury. A significant feature of Mexico's system is the practice (introduced in 1992) of publishing details of failed petitions in the Diario Oficial. This seems to act as a means of inducing potential petitioners to think carefully before filing, and tends to reduce the incidence of frivolous petitions, whose unwelcome side effects may be to harass exporters and importers.

Anti-dumping actions accelerated dramatically between 1991 and 1994, and particularly between 1991 and 1993, when the number of cases initiated increased nine-fold and the number of completed cases three-fold. This may be explained by the strength of the peso and strong import growth. Indeed, preliminary evidence suggests that the number of anti-dumping petitions has fallen significantly in early 1995, following the devaluation of the currency. The tally of 69 anti-dumping and countervailing duties in existence in March 1995 makes Mexico one of the most intensive users of anti-dumping remedies[2] in the world (normalised by the size of trade flows). The intense use of anti-dumping to mitigate the effects on industries of trade liberalisation confers a particular responsibility upon the authorities to ensure that anti-dumping measures do not become pervasive enough to be characterised as a policy reversal or to have unfavourable competitive consequences for user industries.

Most anti-dumping and countervailing investigations between 1987 and March 1995 -- 66 cases, or 35 per cent of the total -- have arisen in the steel sector. This is followed closely by the chemical industry, accounting for 55 cases. Textiles and clothing cases have numbered 19, and the steel, chemicals and textiles and clothing sectors have between them accounted for 63 per cent of all anti-dumping and countervailing investigations initiated. In terms of duties actually imposed, chemical products are the most affected, with 23 cases, followed by 15 for other manufactured products, and 9 each for textiles and clothing, and steel. The relative concentration of anti-dumping and countervailing duty action in the chemicals and steel sectors may reflect the recurrence of unfair trade practices in these products worldwide.

Calculations by the authorities of the incidence of anti-dumping and countervailing duties in terms of an *ad valorem* tariff equivalent which in some cases yield results suggesting rather high margins of protection. Of the 69 anti-dumping and countervailing duty orders in place in March 1995, some 45 per cent of these involved accumulated *ad valorem* duties (the anti-dumping or countervailing duty plus the regular duty) of more than 80 per cent. The highest incidences affected China, ranging up to 1 125 per cent duties for footwear. In effect, anti-dumping actions against a non market economy (China) significantly affect the distribution of duty incidence in an upward direction. A further 19 per cent of the caseload attracted accumulated duties of between 60-80 per cent, 20 per cent duties between 40-60 per cent, and the remaining 16 per cent involved duties of between 10-40 per cent.

The trade coverage of all anti-dumping and countervailing duties in place in March 1995, calculated on the basis of 1994 trade flows, was only 0.5 per cent. This suggests that although Mexico has been a relatively intense user of anti-dumping duties, and the incidence of duties has led to high levels of protection in some cases, the actual trade coverage of the measures remains low. On the other hand, it is important to note that the imposition of duties may be expected to have a strongly inhibiting effect on trade, leading to an understatement of the trade coverage ratio and the real impact of anti-dumping and countervailing duty actions. Two significant outliers as far as the trade coverage ratios are concerned are China and Indonesia, where it is calculated that some 32 per cent and 13 per cent respectively of all Mexican imports from these sources in 1994 were subject to anti-dumping or countervailing duties.

One feature of the Mexican anti-dumping and countervailing duty system that distinguishes it from those of its NAFTA partners is that both the dumping determination and the injury investigation are carried out by the same authorities, i.e SECOFI, whereas in the United States and Canada, these functions are separate. It is unclear that the bifurcation of these functions necessarily improves the system. Indeed, consistency, sound methodology and freedom from political pressure are the most important ingredients of a well-functioning policy "safety valve" in this area, and there is no intrinsic reason for supposing that these objectives cannot be effectively pursued within a single administrative unit. There is a risk that the politicisation of the anti-dumping process might lead to abuse of the system in favour of a more restrictive trade policy. While there is no indication that this is the case at present, it may be desirable to consider the functional separation of anti-dumping from other government functions to ensure its integrity in the future. The treatment of competition policy (see below) provides a precedent for such an approach.

B.   *Safeguards*

Although a general and somewhat vague safeguard provision was introduced into Mexican trade legislation in 1986, it was not until 1993 that a safeguard mechanism was explicitly introduced, in the context of legislative reforms associated with NAFTA. Mexico's safeguard statute is very similar to that of the United States and Canada, and does not appear to raise any legal consistency questions in relation to the WTO Safeguard Agreement. It is important to note that Mexico's 1993 statute conditions a safeguard to the formulation and subsequent implementation of a sectoral adjustment programme. From the petitioner's viewpoint, this raises substantially the cost of activating this kind of measure.

A safeguard instrument may be seen as an alternative to anti-dumping, although for reasons alluded to above concerning the basic difference of premise underlying each kind of measure, the unfair trade remedy of anti-dumping duties is usually preferred by petitioners. Moreover, more stringent standards and greater time-specificity apply in the case of safeguards, making them less attractive to domestic producers seeking relief from import competition. The only safeguard case taken up in Mexico to date was a failed anti-dumping case (fish meal from Chile).

Much the same can be said of the NAFTA safeguard (Article 8) as the multilateral one, at least as far as preference for anti-dumping action is concerned. No safeguard petitions have been filed so far under NAFTA. If producers find options closed off, or encounter greater stringency in the application of anti-dumping and countervailing duty remedies, they may have increasing recourse to safeguards. This may also occur as multilaterally bound duty rates fall and tariffs are removed under free trade agreements.

C.   *Contingency trade policy and competition policy*

As noted earlier, Mexico has made efforts in recent years to broaden participation in anti-dumping and countervailing duty cases, in order to ensure that all interested parties are given a hearing. An extension of this approach involves legal and institutional provisions that permit interaction between the anti-dumping authorities and the competition policy authorities. The Foreign Trade Law empowers SECOFI to inform the Federal Competition Commission of any instances where it considers competition laws may have been breached, or where firms appear to be engaging in monopolistic behaviour. As of March 1995, SECOFI had reported two such cases to the competition authorities. At the same time, the competition policy authorities are entitled to issue opinions concerning any decisions taken by SECOFI involving anti-dumping or countervailing duty actions.

Although the "cross-fertilisation" between anti-dumping and competition policy has barely been tried to date, this may prove in future to be a useful avenue through which to control the monopolistic abuse of market power derived from anti-dumping and countervailing duties. As noted above, the latter actions frequently lead to a severe curtailment of trade in the products concerned, if not to the complete cessation of trade. Where competition is limited in the domestic market, on account of the presence of few producers, it is not difficult to see how significant costs could be visited upon domestic consumers through the use of monopolistic market power.

4.   **Technical standards, marking, labelling and non-preferential rules of origin**

Like anti-dumping and countervailing duties, technical standards, marking and labelling regimes become more important elements of trade policy as a consequence of trade liberalisation. Mexico is no exception in this regard. Mexico's entire standards system underwent a substantial overhaul in 1992, with the introduction of a new law on standards and measurement (Ley Federal sobre Metrología y Normalización). The law established mandatory technical standards (NOM) and voluntary quality standards (NMX). The NOMs cover all areas of economic activity, including products and processes, inputs into production, services, premises, and installations. Some of these are more directly relevant to trade than others. The criteria for deciding to establish NOMs relate to whether a risk exists on account of personal safety and human, animal and plant health, the environment, working conditions, and the preservation of natural resources.

The law establishes a National Standards Commission, supported by a National Standards Consultative Committee. These bodies are responsible for developing and approving NOMs, on the basis of expert recommendations and following ample opportunities for public comment. By early 1995, more than 650 NOMs had been approved, or were at the draft stage for review and public comment. Previously, many old NOMs had been removed from the books, on the grounds that they were in need of updating. More than 5 000 NMXs have also been developed, but on account of their voluntary nature, these are not subject to the same regulatory requirements as NOMs. For the most part, NMXs are designed to help consumers in their purchasing decisions and to exert a positive influence on product and process quality.

Procedures for certification have also been overhauled. All certification activities used to be undertaken by the government, but now several private sector organisations have been granted certification authority. Relatively few of these bodies exist, giving rise to concerns about monopolistic or rent-seeking behaviour on their part, and so local producers and importers still have the right to use the certification services of the government. Importers must obtain compliance certificates if they produce products subject to NOMs. These may be obtained from the competent national authorities, approved foreign authorities, or accredited certification bodies. Certificates are normally valid for six months. One aspect of Mexico's standards regime which has not been extensively developed so far is that of mutual recognition among domestic and foreign certification authorities. It is expected that such facilities will be developed over time. Under NAFTA, there is an obligation to develop mutual recognition arrangements among certification authorities within three years of entry into force of the agreement.

A certain number of complaints have been made about the possible protectionist effects of Mexico's standards regime. Some importers have questioned the need for NOMs in certain cases, arguing for NMXs instead. It appears that the government has strived to ensure that attempts by interested parties to design NOMs for protectionist ends are resisted. Nevertheless some general complaints have been received in the past from trading partners to the effect that certain NOMs are excessively strict. Products mentioned in this connection include electrical goods, tires and wool clothing.

In the area of labelling, marking and non-preferential origin rules, however, affected parties have made a number of complaints concerning the regulations and the manner of their application. Mexico has used NOMs to establish labelling and marking regulations. In particular, NOM-050-SCFI-1994 establishes general packaging and labelling requirements for national and imported goods. NOM-051-SCFI-1994 does likewise specifically for certain food and beverages. Perhaps the most widely made complaint is that the information contained on labels must be affixed before the product concerned arrives in the country. Depending on the goods concerned, this may mean that labelling has to be undertaken at the factory. The inconvenience of such a procedure arises from the fact that labels may be destination-specific, on account of different national labelling requirements, and manufacturers do not always know to where their products are destined. Other complaints have concerned the degree of detailed information required for packaging and labelling purposes, and the fact that verification procedures take place in customs and not at the point of sale, thereby leading to costly delays in clearing goods. The national Chambers of Commerce have also argued that packaging and labelling requirements should be promulgated in a NMX, and not a NOM.

In the area of non-preferential origin rules, Mexico developed a regulation in 1994 which entailed special origin requirements in cases where goods were subject to countervailing or anti-dumping duties. These rules were designed to guard against the circumvention of such duties through various means, including transhipment *via* third countries. For all goods subject to anti-dumping or countervailing duties, certificates of origin are required provided that they may be issued according to the legislation of the country of exportation of the good or of the country where the last major production process took place. For textiles, clothing and footwear, the requirements are more stringent, requiring presentation at the time of importation of the original of a certificate of origin formalised by a competent authority and completed according to specific instructions. These procedures are subject to closer vigilance by the authorities than in respect of other products. For countries not members of the WTO, an additional prerequisite is that certificates of origin must be verified by an approved private inspection company. Some countries are concerned that these measures may have trade-inhibiting effects on such products. Moreover, it should be recalled that these additional requirements have now been reinforced in their protective effects by the recent increase to 35 per cent of import duties on these items from non-preferential sources.

5.   Deregulation, trade facilitation and sectoral policy

A.   *Deregulation*

The Salinas administration followed a comprehensive programme of deregulation that was complemented by some sector-specific programmes and programmes oriented specifically at helping import intensive and exporting industries. At the beginning, administrative efforts were focused on macroeconomic stabilisation. This having been achieved, the focus then turned to reducing the regulatory and bureaucratic burdens on the private sector to allow it to take on its role as engine of economic growth.

The major efforts at deregulation were at the Federal level. In this area, perhaps the most important in terms of trade facilitation was the reform of the regulations and laws controlling the transportation industry. Before deregulation, the transportation industry was subject to local licenses and restrictions that resulted in local monopolies that impeded competition in this service. An example of the inefficiency that resulted from these monopolies was that a shipper that transported goods from one region of the country to another would have to make the return trip empty, thus limiting the use of the national fleet of trucks to a fraction of its capacity. In addition, transportation was subject to permits and controls that lent themselves to corrupt practices. Deregulation established fundamental freedoms in the supply of transportation services which had not existed before, such as: freedom to follow the most convenient route; freedom to transport any material (within the boundary of safety regulations); the elimination of geographic restrictions on loading and unloading; and a number of other provisions that established a greater degree of competition and freedom in the supply of transportation services. Other sectors that experienced comprehensive deregulation included airline services (establishing freedom to choose prices and routes within the country); port services; telecommunications; the petrochemical industry; electricity generation; customs agent services; and a comprehensive deregulation of the financial sector to allow for a more efficient financial intermediation[3].

Under the National Development Plan (1995-2000), the Zedillo administration emphasized the need to deregulate at the state and municipal level to eliminate unnecessary discretion on the part of public officials and to eliminate bureaucratic obstacles, permits, and regulations that inhibit the establishment of enterprises and result in inefficiency and rent seeking. This effort will be complemented by a reform of consumer protection laws and the fiscal framework to simplify the requirements but make them more enforceable.

B.   Trade facilitation

An important complement to the deregulation process is trade facilitation specifically for export industries. The main instrument in this area is the COMPEX, a mechanism designed to address particular problems that exporters face (for example unnecessary regulations, bureaucratic inefficiencies, etc.) in attempting to sell their goods abroad. The COMPEX provides for a series of regional committees that meet every three months to attend to problems that exporters present. An exporter uses the COMPEX to bring these problems to the attention of the government. It is the responsibility of the regional

COMPEX to try to solve the problem in 30 days or less. If this is not possible, then the problem is referred to a national COMPEX committee which is made up of members of the economic cabinet.

The COMPEX mechanism existed in the past administration at a national level. It is the intention of the Zedillo administration to make the COMPEX mechanism much more comprehensive and to extend its reach to small and medium size enterprises, for which purpose it has been extended to the regional level. In addition, there are COMPEX committees for particular exporting functions such as transportation and customs administration.

In addition to the COMPEX mechanism there are specific programmes for the promotion of exporting industries, known as ALTEX and PITEX. The ALTEX programme recognises the contribution of firms with a high level of exports, and gives them special administrative, fiscal and financial treatment. The PITEX programme includes duty drawbacks for firms that have a high level of imported inputs embodied in exports.

Added to these programmes, there are a number of more general objectives that have been laid out in the National Development Plan (1995-2000). These include:

- Taking advantage of Mexico's access to markets in countries that have signed free trade agreements to increase exports and assure exports markets, and continue the process of negotiation of trade agreements with the countries of Central America. In addition, pursue closer trade relations with the countries of Mercosur, the countries of the Pacific Rim, the EU, and Israel.

- To achieve a greater degree of reciprocity in market access for countries with which Mexico does not have a free trade agreement, and to sanction any attempts at unfair trade and fraudulent practices.

- Maintain a stable real exchange rate that promotes exports and the efficient substitution of imports, avoiding an overvaluation of the exchange rate.

- Facilitate and simplify the mechanisms for export promotion and ensure access for exporters to competitive sources of credit through the national development banks, especially to small and medium size firms.

– Change the mechanisms of export promotion where necessary to incorporate small and medium size firms as much as possible.

– Decentralise the operation of export promotion to the state and municipal level.

– Promote access to external (international) financing by domestic exporters.

– Promote the development of customs infrastructure and simplify customs procedures.

– Strengthen the mechanisms for dissemination of information about foreign markets and opportunities for co-investment in the country.

– Increase the degree of competition in those sectors that have been shielded from competition up to now and that affect the performance of other sectors in the economy.

– Move towards a lower dispersion in the tariff structure and a reduction of effective protection in general among sectors and industries within a framework of reciprocity in commercial negotiations.

C.   *Sectoral policy*

The increased market orientation of the Mexican economy, the diminishing role of the state, and growing reliance on external trade, have all been central planks of government policy. Nevertheless, the government has believed it appropriate to support particular activities. As already mentioned above, ALTEX and PITEX seek to support enterprises engaged in exports. Similarly, BANCOMEXT is a foreign trade bank whose primary objectives are to extend financing in support of the trade sector, encourage investment so as to increase exports, modernise production and stimulate diversification in production. The entire maquiladora programme has also been part of an effort to strengthen the foreign trade sector.

Under the Zedillo administration, new emphasis is also being given to small and medium enterprises, in an effort to help them compete effectively in the marketplace. The rationale for singling out small and medium enterprises for attention is that they employ a significant proportion of the workforce, make a positive contribution to a more equitable income distribution, and generate positive externalities for the rest of the economy in terms of skill formation. The main thrust of government support for small and medium enterprises is through training activities and attempts to intensify economic links between small and large enterprises, which would allow small firms to supply inputs to large ones. Small and medium firms are also expected to benefit from the government's trade facilitation and deregulation efforts described above.

It is noteworthy, that these kind of sector-specific initiatives are very different from traditional sectoral policy of the past, the vestiges of which remain in the automobile sector. At least three factors distinguish "modern" sectoral policy from its antecedents. First, it makes minimal use of subsidies, placing emphasis instead on facilitation, including where the government's own bureaucratic machinery acts as an unnecessary obstacle to economic activity. Second, it does not attempt to defend the market positions of incumbent producers whose inability to compete in a changing environment induces them to seek protection from the government. Third, it is not aimed especially at particular sectors, and even less at particular firms, but rather at activities believed to enjoy high private and/or social returns. Thus, in its modern manifestation, sectoral policy does not seek to protect particular industries or firms from import competition. Rather, it seeks to contribute to an "enabling" environment in which business may be conducted. Mexico's policies towards the productive sectors of the economy in recent years have, for the most part, sought to emphasize this more positive and forward-looking approach.

6.   Institutional reform in customs

Mexico's customs reform deserves particular mention on account of the speed with which it was undertaken and the success it represents as an object lesson in institutional reform. It became increasingly clear to the Mexican authorities that the benefits of trade liberalisation would continue to be seriously attenuated if inefficiency and corruption were permitted to persist in the customs service. Several important changes were made in customs procedures and in the administration, starting in 1989. First, a system of self-declaration was adopted, whereby importers were made responsible for their import declarations and duty assessment. Import agents were also made liable in the event of false declarations, except in respect of chemical products and customs valuation for duty purposes. Agents are obligatory for importers, except where firms have their own customs clearing arrangements.

Second, the principle of one hundred per cent physical inspection was dropped. This approach had never been effective, since such a high level of physical examination of cargo is simply impossible without inordinate levels of resources. Nevertheless, the attempt to cover all imports in this manner created long delays in customs and encouraged irregular procedures for securing fast customs clearance. Under the new system, approximately 10 per cent of all cargoes are subject to physical inspection on a random basis, and these inspections are supplemented as appropriate through risk profiling and on the basis of any intelligence received alleging irregularities. Of the 10 per cent of imports inspected on a random basis, 10 per cent is inspected a second time, in this case by a private firm. The purpose of the second inspection is to detect any malfeasance practiced by customs officials in collusion with agents.

A third change was to make customs duties payable in commercial banks, instead of directly to the customs authorities, thereby further cutting down opportunities for illicit collusion between importers or their agents and government officials. The penalties backing up the new customs system are severe. Importers, agents and customs officials may be fined or prosecuted, depending on the severity of the offence. Agents may lose their licenses and customs officials may also face the lesser penalty of dismissal. The results of the reform have been dramatic. The number of employees in the customs service fell from 7 302 in 1989 to 3 306 in 1993, representing a reduction in staff of more than 50 per cent. At the same time, the number of authorised customs agents has been increased from approximately 380 in 1989 to around 800 in 1993, with the objective of ensuring adequate competition among them. Duty collections approximately doubled in the same four-year period, attributable in large measure to improved tax collection efficiency. And most significantly from the point of trade liberalisation, customs clearance times fell from anything up to 24 hours to a few minutes. The maximum time allowed for clearing trucks, except under exceptional circumstances, now stands at three hours.

7.   Privatisation and competition policy

A.   *Privatisation*

During most of Mexico's recent economic development, the predominance of the state in the economy resulted in a growing number of private firms with a strong government interest, parastatal firms, and decentralised government organisations, which took over much of the private sector's role in the production and distribution of goods and services. This trend reached a peak during the administration of José Lopez Portillo (1976-1982), during which the government defined the role of the public sector as the "administration of abundance" of Mexico's new found oil reserves. This resulted in a large increase in government participation in the economy, and ended with the nationalisation of the banking system as a result of the debt crisis in 1982. After the debt crisis, the new administration of Miguel de la Madrid recognised the need to divest the public sector of the many firms in which it had an interest. Between 1982 and 1988, 776 parastatal organisations (defined as organisations that have some government control) were divested, the majority being dissolved, merged with other companies or transferred to private hands. Only a small number were actually sold, so that the proceeds from divestiture during this period remained below US$500 million.

It was not until 1989 that the reprivatisation of the largest firms and organisations that were in the hands of the government (including the banking sector) began. By the end of 1991 these included the two major airlines (Aereomexico and Mexicana de Aviacion), one of the largest copper mining companies in the world (Compañía Minera de Cananea), Sidermex (the largest steel mill complex in Mexico), and Telefonos de México (TELMEX), the national communications monopoly. In 1992 the privatisation of the banking system was completed putting 18 commercial banks back in the hands of the private sector. By 1993, the parastatal sector, which had at one time had 1 155 organisations under its control, was reduced to 213 organisations (Table 19).

Aside from its comprehensive nature, the success of the Mexican privatisation programme lies in its effect on public finances. Government receipts from privatisation were considerable, reaching a magnitude of 4.32 per cent of government revenues and 1.19 per cent of GDP in 1990 and 14.4 per cent of government revenues and 3.83 per cent of GDP in 1991 (this last mainly due to the sale of TELMEX). Recognising that this was a one-shot increase in government income, a contingency fund was created outside the regular government budget to hold the proceeds of privatisation. This fund was originally to be used to counteract the effects of unforeseen economic events such as a drastic decline in the price of petroleum on international markets. Given the stability of petroleum prices by 1991, however, the government decided to use the proceeds from the fund to retire 20 billion pesos of domestic government debt, reducing the level of domestic public debt in that year to 18.4 per cent of GDP, well below that for the majority of OECD countries. In June of 1992, proceeds from the fund and other sources were used to cancel US$7.181 billion of foreign debt, with corresponding savings in terms of interest payments. The privatisation programme further helped government finances by eliminating the need for the large subsidies that the public sector injected into many of the parastatal enterprises. Thus the principle benefit of the Mexican privatisation programme was its contribution to the creation of stable macroeconomic conditions through its effect in helping to balance government finances.

The Zedillo administration has maintained privatisation initiatives as part of the government economic policy. These have been broadened given the further need to cut back on government finances. The major initiatives in this respect are the privatisation of the national railway company (Ferrocarriles Nacionales de México), the major ports, the generation of electricity, and some of the downstream activities of the national petroleum monopoly (PEMEX).

B.   Competition policy

Privatisation and deregulation were oriented towards increasing the role of competition in the Mexican economy, in effect substituting the many regulations that the state imposed on the private sector with the disciplines of competition in the internal and external market. With this policy, however, there arose the danger of the prevalence of unfair competition in the form of the exercise of monopoly power, collusion or other price fixing arrangements. The legal structure in Mexico to restrict monopolistic power was put in place in the 1930s, but was nullified by a series of regulations imposed two years after the law was introduced. As a result, Mexico had no effective competition policy until the new Federal Economic Competition Law (Ley Federal de Competencia Económica - LFCE) was instituted in 1993.

The LFCE establishes a Federal Competition Commission (CFC), independent of any branch of the government, to implement the law. The CFC is formed by five commissioners, named by the President of the Republic for a period of 10 years, one to be replaced in a staggered fashion every two years.

The CFC has the faculties to pursue the investigations necessary and to make all determinations in terms of competition law, without intervention from the Executive or the Judicial powers.

The LFCE establishes two types of anticompetitive behaviour characterised as "absolute" and "relative" monopoly practices. Absolute monopoly practices constitute agreements among competitors. Those include price fixing agreements, agreements to fix bids in auction processes, agreements to restrict output to influence market price or market sharing arrangements. These are considered to have a negative effect on competition and are sanctioned outright irrespective of the market power of the incumbent firms. Relative monopoly practices, on the other hand, are restrictions imposed by firms on non competitors such as distributors or clients, in order to avoid entrance from other competitor firms or to establish anticompetitive exclusivity advantages. However, those vertical restrictions may be either efficient and pro-competitive or harmful to competition and their effect depend on the specific case involved. These practices include exclusivity agreements among companies and distributors, which may increase the quality of service offered in conjunction with the product, but which could also result in the unfair exclusion of other competitors in the distribution system. Other relative monopoly practices include restrictions on the resale price of a good, sales tied to certain conditions of supply, boycotts, refusal to deal with a particular firm goods and services normally offered to others, and in general to any vertical agreement that may harm competition. However, a condition to sanction a relative monopoly practice is that the incumbent firms have substantial market power in the relevant market, according to the criteria provided by the LFCE.

In addition to anti-competitive practices, the LFCE also give the CFC the obligation to review mergers and acquisitions to avoid uncompetitive concentration in particular industries. Mergers and acquisitions are subject to review if they meet any of three conditions:

- If the transaction value exceeds 12 million times the current minimum wage in the Federal District.

- If the transaction or series of transactions involved leads one firm to gain control of 35 per cent or more of the assets or shares of another firm whose assets or annual sales exceed the equivalent of 12 million times the current minimum wage in the Federal District.

– The transaction involves two or more firms whose annual sales or assets together add up to more than 48 million times the current minimum wage in the Federal District, and that this transactions will result in the accumulation of additional assets or shares exceeding 4.8 million times the current minimum wage in the Federal District.

The Commission also evaluates allegations of non competitive behaviour of economic agents by individuals or organisations, and receives and answers questions about competition law from private companies and organisations, and can start *ex-officio* research in these sectors where there are signals of anticompetitive behaviour of agents. On the other hand, the Commission has the mandate to comment on any plan or programme of the Federal Government that might affect the level of competition in any particular industry and can comment on the effects of competition of any law, regulation or government administrative practice whenever this is considered relevant for competition.

The CFC began operating in June 1993 and during its first year was active in all areas of its mandate. The three principal areas of work were the analysis of mergers and concentrations, *ex-officio* investigations of monopoly behaviour, and the evaluation of allegations of anti-competitive behaviour by private individuals and organisations. Of these, by far the most important was the evaluation of mergers, of which 86 were notified to the Commission and resolved, the majority without any objection. During its first year the Commission took on 16 *ex-officio* investigations of monopoly behaviour and received 22 denunciations of anticompetitive practices.

A number of highly visible cases have been examined and ruled upon by the Commission. It has investigated the existence of collusion among the main national banks that issue credit cards in fixing commissions charged to establishments in which the cards can be used, and the rates of interest charged to credit card-holders. This case was resolved by an agreement on the part of financial institutions to eliminate information exchange to set commissions paid by establishments and to abstain from agreements with other banks to fix interest rates to card-holders. In another case, the Commission investigated the regulations involved in establishing service stations for the distribution of gasoline set up by PEMEX, the national energy monopoly. These contained geographic restrictions on the number of Gasoline stations that can be opened in a specific area, and distance requirements that may exist between stations, which were determined to be anticompetitive by the Commission. As a result, PEMEX agreed to eliminate those restrictions in order to reduce the distance that consumers need to drive for gasoline and to improve, through further competition, the services provided by gasoline stations. Addressing cases like these has earned the Commission a certain amount of credibility among both government and private sectors. However, the Commission has not been free of criticism or controversy. One criticism refers to the changes that resulted when previous commissioners took positions in the new administration. The allegation is that these changes detract from the credibility of the Commission as an independent institution with a measure of continuity. More recently, the Commission was involved in the evaluation of a merger between TELMEX, the private telephone monopoly, and a division of TELEVISA, the country's largest television company, that offers cable services. It was argued that this represented a monopolistic merger between the two of the largest private firms in the country to exclude others from entering into the lucrative cable communications market. The Commission pronounced that the merger between telecommunications and cable companies was an international trend that enhanced the ability of domestic firms to face international competition. The Commission thus considered that there were no anticompetitive dangers and allowed it to stand.

8.   Investment policy

Up until the early to mid-1980s, Mexico retained rigorous restrictions on FDI. This policy changed at the same time as trade liberalisation began to set in. Indeed, it would have made little sense to open up to trade without relaxing controls on foreign investment, particularly in a modernising economy, where trade and investment are increasingly complementary means of gaining access to markets. Moreover, if Mexico had continued to maintain stringent restrictions on FDI, it would have received less foreign exchange in the form of capital inflows, obtained less funds to help finance the privatisation programme, perhaps also lost opportunities for technology transfer, and more generally, foregone income and employment growth associated with higher levels of investment.

Several changes were made to the Foreign Investment Law, in part through regulatory changes, from 1984 onwards, all in the direction of relaxing FDI restrictions. In 1993, a new Foreign Investment Law was introduced, which sought to offer legal certainty and transparent rules to foreign investors and their investments, in accordance with Constitutional requirements relating to the ownership and control of certain assets. These moves to liberalise FDI, among other factors, contributed to the rapid expansion in FDI registered by

Mexico in recent years (Chapter 2). The new law opened up further branches of economic activities to FDI, reduced the role of the National Commission of Foreign Investment in exercising discretionary powers over investment authorisations, further developed the concept of "neutral investment," whereby foreign capital could participate in an enterprise without enjoying the usual voting rights of equity shareholders, and reduced and simplified the number of administrative steps required for investment approval.

Under the new law, foreign investment is permitted in any sector unless it is specifically mentioned as being subject to restrictions. Restricted sectors include petroleum, certain petrochemical industries, electricity, nuclear energy generation, radioactive minerals, satellite communications, certain transport services, and a range of other service activities. Restrictions take different forms, from outright prohibition to ceilings on equity participation. A number of FDI restrictions have been removed or relaxed in recent years, and overall, the FDI regime is very similar to what is contained in NAFTA and, in some cases, introduces liberalisation going beyond these commitments. A notable feature of Mexico's FDI regime is the absence of the kinds of incentives that so many governments offer through fiscal and other means to attract foreign investors. Given the distortions that such incentives may introduce, and in view of the fact that their effectiveness in influencing investment decisions is open to some doubt, the absence of a FDI incentive package would appear to make good economic sense.

NOTES

1   According to Article 131 of the Constitution of the United Mexican States concerning foreign trade, according to the unfair trade regulation and according to the General Agreement on Tariffs and Trade.

2   Mexico has not used countervailing duties with the same intensity as some other countries, notably the United States.

3   For a comprehensive description of deregulation efforts see Gabriel Martinez and Guillermo Farber, *Desregulación económica (1989-1993),* Fondo de Cultura Económica, Mexico D.F., 1994. For deregulation in the financial sector see Catherine Mansell Carstens, *Las Nuevas Finanzas en Mexico*, ITAM, Mexico D.F., 1994 and Pedro Aspe Armella, *El camino mexicano de la transformación económica,* Fondo de Cultura Económica, México D.F., 1994.

CHAPTER 4

THE NORTH AMERICAN FREE TRADE AGREEMENT AND OTHER REGIONAL TRADE AGREEMENTS

The North American Free Trade Agreement (NAFTA) between Mexico, the United States and Canada went into effect on 1 January 1994. It has been universally hailed as a historic trade agreement, the first regional integration agreement to be signed between advanced industrial nations and a developing nation, and in its principles and scope the most ambitious effort of its kind. Rather than negotiating on the basis of sector specific requirements for protection, NAFTA started from an agreement among the parties on the benefits of liberalisation and the WTO sanctioned principles of market access with national treatment and most-favoured nation (MFN) treatment. These principles led to a very broad scope of action in the negotiations, including major manufacturing sectors, services, government procurement, trade-related investment measures, intellectual property rights, a dispute settlement procedure and the reform of Mexico's investment regime. In addition, the three countries entered into co-operation agreements on two new issues relative to labour standards and environmental protection, that had not before been so explicitly considered before.

For Mexico, NAFTA performs various important functions. As mentioned in Chapter 2, by codifying many of liberalisation initiatives, the evolution towards a more liberal trade and investment regime has been assured. The trade agreement safeguards these developments from future reversals and lends an air of credibility to the government's policy initiatives. In this respect it was an integral part of the government's strategy to attract FDI and repatriated capital, along with privatisation and debt reduction. NAFTA also assures Mexico preferential access to the US market, its closest trading partner and largest source of foreign capital. And, as mentioned in Chapter 2, NAFTA has provided a model for FTAs that Mexico has signed with other countries in Latin America (reviewed below).

NAFTA is comprehensive in nature, although it is not a customs union with a common external tariff, and neither is it intended that it should become a common market. In consequence, such questions as the free movement of labour are not addressed, and certain sensitive sectors are omitted from the agreement, including petroleum extraction and refining. In one or two areas, such as motor vehicles and textiles and clothing, rules of origin require a significant transformation in this region by restricting duty free treatment only to products that meet the definition of originating goods. However, this feature of NAFTA, however, does not depend on whether NAFTA is designed as a free trade area, or as some other kind of agreement -- it simply reflects specific policy towards sensitive sectors, of a kind found in many other countries around the world.

This chapter briefly reviews NAFTA, highlighting the main features of the Agreement and their implications for how liberal Mexico's trade policy is becoming[1]. Progress in the implementation of the Agreement is then reviewed, as well as the preliminary result in terms of trade and investment for the first year of implementation. A final section looks at Mexico's FTAs with other countries.

1.   The North American Free Trade Agreement

This section provides a summary of the main provisions of the Agreement, with particular emphasis on what has been left out or what remains to be implemented[2] The Agreement provides for the immediate elimination of tariffs on a number of goods and the elimination of tariffs and non-tariff barriers on substantially all trade over ten years. In addition, it liberalises considerably some key sectors of services trade such as transportation, telecommunications and professional services, and allows for mutual access to government procurement contracts. It liberalises Mexico's foreign investment regime considerably, sets up common standards for competition policy, and implements disciplines on government technical standards and sanitary and phytosanitary measures. What follows is a brief review of provisions in the more important sectors covered by the Agreement.

A.   *Sectoral agreements*

a)   *Agriculture*

Separate agreements were signed by Mexico with the United States and Canada under the NAFTA to liberalise agricultural trade. Under the US-Mexico Agreement, tariffs on products that made up 57 per cent of US-Mexico farm trade in 1993 were eliminated at the time the Agreement went into force (January 1994). Using 1994 weights, tariffs on the products that made up a subsequent 6 per cent of trade will be eliminated five years after the implementation, an additional 32 per cent in ten years, and the final 5 per cent in fifteen years. Non-tariff barriers, mainly quotas and import licenses, will be transformed into tariff rate quotas and eliminated over ten to fifteen years. Given the previous structure of protection, this progressive liberalisation gives US consumers greater access to Mexican horticultural products (tomatoes, melons and oranges), sugar and cotton, while Mexican consumers will have greater access to US grains and field crops (principally corn, dry beans and potatoes). The Agreement contemplates the creation of a working group to examine liberalisation of agricultural export subsidies, however no specific commitments in this area appear in NAFTA.

b)   *Automobiles*

The automobile and auto parts industry is one of the most integrated industry across borders in North America, and makes up the largest component of bilateral trade between the United States and Mexico and between Mexico and Canada. NAFTA will further facilitate the integration of this industry by allowing for significant reductions in tariff and non-tariff barriers. All tariffs on vehicles and auto parts will be phased out over a period of ten years. At the time the Agreement went into effect, Mexico lowered its tariff on autos from 20 to 10 per cent, the remaining to be phased out over ten years. Tariffs on heavy and light trucks will also be phased out over five years. The United States eliminated all tariffs on autos, halved the tariff on trucks, and will phase these out by 1999. For auto parts, the bulk of tariffs will be phased out over five years.

Measures relative to the automobile industry on the Mexican side principally consist of domestic content and trade balancing requirements and import quotas for heavy vehicles. Regional value requirements will be reduced from 34 per cent in 1994 to 29 per cent in 1999, and zero by the year 2004, with a decreasing portion of growth in the Mexican market guaranteed for Mexican auto parts producers. When the Agreement came into effect, trade balancing requirements were reduced from US$2 of exports for every dollar imported to 80 cents. These will be brought down to 55 cents in 2003 and eliminated in 2004. In addition, in January 1994 Mexico lifted its quota on new auto imports (15 per cent of the market), but quotas on trucks and busses will apply for five years.

Under this liberalisation process, there are provisions relative to the automobile industry, like the rules of origin, that promote further integration between the three countries' auto industries. For vehicles, engines and transmissions, rules of origin dictate 50 per cent of net cost of production to come from North American made inputs for the first four years of the Agreement, 56 per cent for the second four years, and 62.5 per cent thereafter. For other auto parts the requirement is 60 per cent. Therefore during the transition period, it will become more difficult for autos and auto parts originating from non-NAFTA countries to qualify for the duty free treatment.

Another aspect of the automobile chapter is the slow liberalisation of the market for used cars. The Mexican prohibition on imports of used cars will remain for fifteen years and after that will be phased out over a ten-year period. In the circumstances, this means that Mexican consumers will not be able to benefit fully from access to the US or Canadian used car markets until 25 years after NAFTA goes into effect.

c)   *Textiles and clothing*

The main issue in the textiles and clothing negotiations for Mexico was increased access to the US market. In this respect, the provisions for textiles and clothing under NAFTA provide for the elimination of tariff and non-tariff barriers and the establishment of very strict rules of origin, preserving the opportunities of the increase in trade for North American producers. The rules of origin are "yarn-forward" and "fiber-forward", meaning that to qualify for NAFTA preferences textiles and apparel must be made from yarn spun in North America or from textiles fabricated from North America fibers. This essentially covers most of the products in the textile and apparel industry, since the spinning of yarn and the production of fibers occur at the very initial stages of production.

For textiles and clothing that comply with the rules of origin, the restrictive quotas that were in place against Mexican exports to the United States under the Multifibre Arrangement will be eliminated immediately, for originating goods, and a schedule for elimination is provided for the remaining quotas on non-originating products (14 categories). No new quotas may be imposed except under the safeguard provisions (see below). Specific products that do not meet NAFTA rules of origin can still quality for preferential treatment up to a specified import level or "tariff preference level" which is negotiated among the three countries.

d)   *Energy and petrochemicals*

In contrast to textiles and apparel, the main issue in energy and petrochemicals was access by US and Canadian capital to Mexico's energy sector. On this count, NAFTA disappointed many observers by not eliminating restrictions on investment and private participation in Mexico's petroleum industry. Nevertheless, it did open up the sector moderately to foreign investment. Under NAFTA Mexico lifted restrictions on 14 of the 19 previous basic petrochemicals categories and on all secondary petrochemicals, opened up self-generation, co-generation and independent production of electricity to foreign investors, and entirely liberalised coal mining. Mexico also agreed to eliminate half of all tariffs on oil and gas field equipment and coal, and phase out the others over five to ten years. However, oil exploration, production and refining, as well as gasoline retailing and any trade in gasoline are still reserved for PEMEX, Mexico's public energy monopoly, and trade in electricity is also reserved for the Federal Electricity Commission (FEC), Mexico's public distribution monopoly.

The main benefit of liberalisation in this sector lies not in foreign investment, but rather in Mexico's opening up of the lucrative procurement contracts in the energy and petroleum sector to foreign suppliers. When NAFTA went into effect 50 per cent of PEMEX and FEC procurement contracts were opened up to foreign participation. After ten years the figure will be 100 per cent. In 1993 PEMEX contracts represented US$5.5 billion while FEC contracts were worth US$3 billion.

e)   *Financial services*

In financial services NAFTA opens up the Mexican market considerably to investment by US and Canadian firms, but with market share restrictions up until the year 2000. Foreign banks are allowed to enter the Mexican market with an 8 per cent share in 1995, increasing to 15 per cent in 1999 and 100 per cent in 2000. However, Mexico can impose a one-time three year restriction on further acquisitions of US and Canadian banks between 2000 and 2004 if the NAFTA partner's share is over 25 per cent. In addition, no single bank will be allowed to have more than 1.5 per cent of the market until the year 2000, with a cap of 4 per cent thereafter.

Insurance is one of the more attractive areas of liberalisation for US and Canadian firms, Mexico being a substantially underinsured market with great potential for growth. There are substantial limitations on cross-border sales of insurance (except re-insurance), but entry is permitted through joint ventures with Mexican firms.

Brokerages will be open to foreign ownership, initially limited to 10 per cent of the market, but rising up to 30 per cent by the end of the transition period. Individual foreign-owned brokerages will be allowed to a maximum share of 4 per cent to be lifted after the transition period.

f)   *Transportation*

By far the largest component of trade within NAFTA is transported across land, so liberalisation of land transportation was a key issue in the Agreement. NAFTA provides a timetable for removing barriers to cross-border trade in land transportation and for establishing compatible technical and safety standards. Most of the restrictions to land transportation services will be eliminated six years after the Agreement has gone into effect. When the Agreement went into effect free access was granted to charter and tour bus services between the United States and Mexico. Three years after the Agreement is implemented (1997) the NAFTA will allow US and Canadian bus firms to begin scheduled service to and from any part of Mexico, with the same treatment going for Mexican bus firms in the United States. Six years after the Agreement is implemented (by the end of 1999) US, Mexican and Canadian trucking companies will have access to all the United States and Mexico both for pick-up and delivery.

NAFTA also allows for investment in transportation services among signatories, with subsidiaries allowed three years after implementation, minority ownership by 1999 and unrestricted ownership in the year 2004. In addition, NAFTA has some provisions that allow foreign investment in ports but no provisions for investment in rail. However, this restriction was recently overturned by the Zedillo administration, which is seeking to privatise the national railroad company, Ferrocarriles Nacionales de México (FERRONALES).

g)   Telecommunications

The liberalisation of telecommunications services is essential for improved performance of the telecommunications sector and for increased exchange of data and information in the integration of financial services. Mexico has already privatised its telephone monopoly (TELMEX), which has advanced in the arduous task of replacing most of Mexico's outdated telephone network. NAFTA adds to these efforts by liberalising most value added services, allowing the establishment of private networks, eliminating tariffs on trade in telecommunications equipment, and establishing principles that allow equal and fair access to public networks.

Much of the liberalisation in NAFTA has been implemented by a new telecommunications law that was passed in early May 1995. The law allows for private investment in long-distance services, local value added services, and local non-wire services. The law clears the way for Mexico to begin to select the private companies (most of them joint ventures between US telephone companies and large Mexican conglomerates) that will receive concessions for local non-wire and long-distance service.

h)   Maquiladora industry

The maquiladora industry is expected to shrink in the coming years, and perhaps eventually disappear under NAFTA. Firms on the Mexico-US border will tend to become more integrated into the Mexican economy. Under the Agreement, duty drawbacks on non-NAFTA components will disappear by 2001, and Mexico will eliminate the 50 per cent limitation on sales of maquiladoras into the Mexican market over seven years. In addition, domestic content and trade balancing requirements were completely eliminated when the Agreement went into effect.

i)   *Cross border trade in services and temporary movement of business persons*

The provisions for cross-border trade in services in NAFTA establish basic rules and obligations to facilitate trade in services between the three countries. It does not apply to activities such as government procurement, subsidies, financial or energy related services covered in other parts of the Agreement, as well as air services, basic telecommunications, government provided social services and the maritime industry. In addition, sectors reserved by the Mexican Constitution for the Mexican State or Mexican Nationals are excluded[3].

The Agreement extends the concepts of national treatment and MFN treatment to services. Under these rules each NAFTA country must treat service providers from the other NAFTA countries no less favourably than it treats its own service providers or providers from other countries that receive MFN status (whichever is most favourable)[4]. In addition, under that Agreement a NAFTA country may not require a service provider of another NAFTA country to establish or maintain a residence, representative office, branch or any other form of enterprise (local presence) in its territory as a condition for the provision of service. There is an exception to these rules which allows each country to keep certain federal, state and local laws that violate national or MFN treatment, as long as they are listed and other members of the treaty are advised within two years of implementation. This proviso refers especially to state and local government measures. Each country will also list existing non-discriminatory measures that limit the number of service providers or the operations of service providers in a particular sector. Consultations and future liberalisation of such measures is contemplated in the Agreement.

The Services section of the Agreement also establishes provisions related to professional licensing and certification designed to avoid unnecessary barriers to trade. Under NAFTA, each country must ensure that its licensing and certification procedures are based on objective and transparent criteria, and that they are no more burdensome than is necessary to ensure the quality of the service[5]. A process for eventual mutual recognition of licenses and certification is provided for in principle under the Agreement, but such recognition is not required as a part of trade liberalisation. As part of the Agreement the three countries will undertake a work programme for liberalisation of licensing of foreign legal consultants and temporary licensing of engineers. Two years after the Agreement is in place all residency or citizenship requirements for licensing and certification will be eliminated. In order to qualify for NAFTA benefits, a non-NAFTA service provider must have a substantive business activity within a NAFTA country. For transportation firms NAFTA benefits are reserved for those providers whose equipment is registered in a NAFTA country.

Related to cross-border services there are provisions in the Agreement for the temporary movement of business persons. While the NAFTA does not create a common market, it seeks to facilitate the movement of business persons within the territories. For this purpose the countries will grant temporary entry to four categories of business persons: business visitors, traders, intra-company transferees, and certain categories of professionals.

B. Trade rules

a) Rules of origin

Rules of origin aim to preserve the preferential treatment of trade for the members of the Agreement and to avoid triangulation of trade from non-NAFTA countries to obtain preferential access to NAFTA markets. Under NAFTA, goods will qualify for preferential treatment if they are wholly obtained or produced in North America, or if they fulfil certain conditions that confer NAFTA origin. These conditions may vary across products but essentially fall under two specific types: transformation or regional value tests. Under a transformation test, a good that contains inputs from non-NAFTA countries must have undergone sufficient transformation to change tariff classification under the HS. Under the regional value test, a good must include a certain percentage of NAFTA countries measured as a percentage of the transaction value of the good (value added) or a percentage of the net cost of production of the good (excluding cost of royalties, sales promotion, packing and shipping, and limiting the cost of interest). This test applies to sensitive products in the Agreement like automobiles, As a final provision, if a good fails to meet a specific rule of origin, it will still be considered of North American origin if the value of non-NAFTA materials in the good makes up no more than 7 per cent of the price or net cost of the product.

b)　　*Anti-dumping and countervailing duties*

This section of the Agreement is largely modelled after the Canada-US Free Trade Agreement provisions of anti-dumping and countervailing duties. NAFTA establishes a mechanism for the review of final national anti-dumping and countervailing duty determinations by an independent binational panel, and sets procedures for panel review of changes to each country's anti-dumping and countervailing duty laws. In addition, it establishes an "extraordinary challenge" procedure to deal with allegations that certain actions may have affected a panel's decision and the panel review process. Finally the NAFTA creates a safeguard mechanism designed to remedy instances in which application of a country's domestic law undermines the functioning of the panel process[6].

c)　　*Dispute settlement*

This section is also modelled after the dispute settlement procedures of the Canada-US FTA. A trilateral Trade Commission comprising cabinet level representatives from each country is established to administer the Agreement and adjudicate disputes over the interpretation or application of NAFTA rules. The Commission will facilitate consultations on trade disputes, but if these consultations do not result in a resolution then the dispute will be heard by an arbitral panel. Alternatively, if the dispute can also be brought under the GATT then the complaining country has the choice between GATT resolution mechanisms and NAFTA. Once one is chosen, the forum cannot be changed.

Once the panel comes to a decision on the dispute, it will forward its recommendations to the disputing countries who will come to an agreement. If a panel determines that a country has acted in a manner inconsistent with its NAFTA obligations, and the disputing countries do not reach an agreement, the complaining country may suspend the application of equivalent NAFTA benefits until the issue is resolved. Any country that considers the retaliation to be excessive may obtain a panel ruling on this question.

d)　　*Safeguards*

The safeguard provisions in NAFTA allow for the implementation of temporary protection under specified circumstances. To a large extent they follow GATT practice, but in some respects are more stringent. Similar to GATT, under NAFTA rules, partners can impose a safeguard if, as a result of NAFTA, increased imports constitute a "substantial cause or threat" of "serious injury" to the industry in question. However, a safeguard action can be taken only once and for a maximum period of three years (four years in the case of some industries). Bilateral safeguard actions can be taken after the transition period only with the consent of the exporting country.

The actions that can be taken in the case of a safeguard include the suspension of further reductions in tariffs or the re-establishment of the previous tariff (snap back). The partner taking the action must compensate the other country in the form of a trade concession equal in value to the lost trade because of the safeguard. If the countries cannot come to an agreement on this previous point the exporting country may impose trade measures of equivalent effect on the importing country. Finally, when a country takes a safeguard action on a global or multilateral basis, it must exclude all NAFTA partners, unless these make up a significant proportion of the trade in the product. A significant proportion is considered to be within the top five suppliers of the good in question.

In addition to these global safeguards there are special safeguard provision for sensitive sectors such as agriculture and textiles and apparel. In agriculture there are tariff rate quotas that can be imposed for sensitive products which, for Mexico include pork, apples, potatoes, barley and malt. In textiles and apparel there is a special causation test (serious damage or actual threat of serious damage) that will apply.

e)　　*Technical standards*

The signatories of the NAFTA recognise in the Agreement that it is necessary to maintain certain standards-related measures to ensure safety, and the protection of human, animal and plant life and health, as well as protection of the environment and consumers. The Agreement contains disciplines related to standards designed to facilitate trade between the three countries. The main provisions of these disciplines is national treatment and MFN treatment for other NAFTA countries with relation to standards. In addition, the Agreement sets out a detailed list of rules governing procedures for assessing compliance with standards, so that these do not create unnecessary obstacles to trade. The Agreement also sets up a Committee on Standards-Related Measures to monitor the implementation of this part of the Agreement and to investigate harmonisation of standards among NAFTA countries.

C.   Trade related issues

a)   Investment provisions

It is widely recognised that the most significant gains from the NAFTA for Mexico (and indeed for all participants) will come from the rationalisation of production that results from the liberalisation of investment rules. Hence the investment provisions of the Agreement are an important part of the package. Many of the sector chapters contain provisions opening up industries to foreign investment. The chapter on investment thus lays down a framework for the treatment of foreign firms in general, establishing that NAFTA investors will receive national treatment (meaning treatment equal to that of national investors in the host country), or MFN treatment (treatment accorded to most favoured trading or investment partners), whichever is most favourable. In addition, existing performance requirements (for example dealing with regional value, trade balancing or technology transfer) are eliminated over the transition period, and new performance requirements are prohibited.

Some of the provisions of the NAFTA chapter on investment are significant because they greatly reduce the restrictions on foreign investment in Mexico, making it a much more attractive market for foreign firms. For example, the right of expropriation is limited only to actions that have an explicit public purpose, and just and prompt compensation is assured in these cases. In addition, the NAFTA countries have pledged to allow the free flow of capital without restrictions, and guaranteed access to hard currency. NAFTA permits each country to impose its own pollution abatement and other environmental technology requirements. Finally, the Agreement puts in place detailed dispute settlement procedures under which investment disputes go to binding, enforceable international arbitration, with strict limits on further action through domestic legal systems.

There are some exceptions to these general rules. They do not apply to Mexico's energy or rail sectors (although as mentioned above, since the 1994 crisis the rail sector has been opened to foreign investment), the US airlines and radio communications, and Canada's cultural industries. There are also exemptions for some state and local measures, government procurement, export promotion, and foreign aid activities. The restrictions that have been codified in other chapters of the Agreement also apply during the transition period (i.e. Mexico's restrictions on market share and industry participation in the financial sector).

In addition to the investment provisions, an important component of the investment agreements is a US-Mexico tax treaty that significantly reduces the withholding rates charged on interest, dividends and royalties flowing between the two countries.

b)   Intellectual property rights

NAFTA's provisions on intellectual property also greatly enhance Mexico's attractiveness as a host for foreign investments by locking in reforms in the intellectual property regime codified in Mexico's 1991 Intellectual Property Rights Law. It provides broad protection of copyrights, trademarks, industrial designs and geographic appellations, as well as patents and trade secrets.

c)   Competition policy

To fulfil the objectives of the Agreement, the NAFTA includes provisions that restrict anticompetitive practices by both government and private businesses. The main provision of the Agreement commits each country to maintain measures against anticompetitive business practices and to co-operate with the other countries on issues of competition law enforcement.

d)   Government procurement

NAFTA establishes access to a country's government procurement contracts over a certain size. For procurement by federal government departments and agencies NAFTA companies can bid for procurement over

US$50 000 for goods and services and US$6.5 million for construction services. For federal government enterprises the figures are: over US$250 million for goods and services and US$8 million for construction services. Mexico will phase in its coverage over ten years (see Energy and petrochemicals above).

e)   *Accession*

The accession clause in NAFTA provides for admitting any country or group of countries into NAFTA. However, the criteria and procedures for application and acceptance of accession are not spelled out in the Agreement, therefore it remains to be seen how the accession clause will work out in practice. In this respect, the ongoing process of accession of Chile to NAFTA will throw the first light into the functioning of the accession clause.

f)   *The Side Agreements*

In addition to the main body of the Agreement, which was negotiated by the end of 1992, the NAFTA parties negotiated co-operation agreements in 1993, pertaining to the environment (the North American Agreement on Environmental Co-operation -- NAAEC), labour (the North American Agreement on Labour Co-operation -- NAALC), and an additional understanding on import surges (Understanding Between the Parties to the North American Free Trade Agreement Concerning Chapter Eight -- Import Surges).

The Side Agreements on the environment and labour provide for the establishment of two commissions (The Commission on Environmental Co-operation and the Commission on Labour Co-operation) to oversee the process of law enforcement. Under these Side Agreements each country committed to effectively enforce its environmental and labour laws. Thus, complaints to the Commissions will be pertaining to situations where one country alleges that another has failed in this respect. Under the Labour Agreement, the complaints will be referred to one of three National Administrative Offices for resolution at the local level before they go to the Commission. Environmental complaints may be raised on a wide variety of issues. Labour issues address two different groups of issues with different measures. In the first group refers to occupational health and safety, child labour, and minimum wages, for which violations will be subject to fines and trade measures. The second group includes disputes related to migrant workers, forced labour, employment discrimination, equal pay for men and women, compensation in cases of work accidents and occupational diseases. Infractions in this group will only be subject to official consultations and review by independent experts. Disputes in these areas can only be the subject of consultations at the ministerial level.

Under the Side Agreements, disputes will be taken up by councils within the Commissions, where evaluations and plans for resolution will be accorded. If the action plans are not fully implemented, the arbitration panels in the Commissions can determine fines to be levied, or as a last resort, may include trade measures.

g)   *Understanding on import surges*

The Understanding on Import Surges establishes a new mechanism for monitoring trade that will allow for the anticipation of rapid and harmful increases in imports before the problem becomes severe enough to elicit industry complaints. The aim is to establish an early warning system through constant monitoring of trade flows and domestic market conditions. Aside from this proviso, the Agreement does not contemplate any safeguard mechanisms beyond those already in place in the main body of the Agreement. As an addendum, this Understanding establishes a working group to evaluate how well the safeguard provisions in NAFTA are functioning.

h)   *Border infrastructure*

An innovative mechanism for financing border infrastructure development was created under NAFTA. This mechanism is innovative because it is regionally and locally based -- focusing exclusively on the problems of the border area --, because it is binational in nature -- involving planning and financing from both the Mexican and the US side, and because it represents a unique combination of efforts by both the private and the public sector. This mechanism is established under the Border Environment Co-operation Commission, based in El Paso, which will help border states and communities design and arrange financing for priority environmental infrastructure projects, and the North American Development Bank (NADBank), which will use public capital from both the Mexican and the US governments to leverage private financing for border development.

i)   *Border Environment Co-operation Commission*

The Border Environment Co-operation Commission will act as a clearing house for border environment infrastructure projects. It has a binational Board of Directors with federal, state and local government representation from both the United States and Mexico. It also has a public advisory council, with members drawn from the border region, to provide for public notice and comment on proposed border infrastructure projects. The Commission will work in the following manner; for example if the City of El Paso seeks to expand its wastewater treatment facility, it will approach the Border Environment Co-operation Commission for assistance. The Commission will be able to provide El Paso with access to considerable expertise in planning, designing, constructing and operating the facility, and assessing its economic benefits. In addition, the Commission will serve as a conduit for improving coordination among the various groups and jurisdictions on both sides of the border that have an interest in the results of the project. For example, the Commission might encourage El Paso to include its sister city in Mexico, Ciudad Juárez, in the planning process to help ensure that mutual concerns are addressed and, where appropriate, economies of scale in design, construction, and operations are considered.

Once the project is ready for formal review, it will go to the Advisory Council of the Commission for comment and then to the Board of Directors for certification. Each project would have to meet local environmental requirements. Project proposals which will affect both sides of the border will go through an environmental assessment. The public will also be able to comment on all projects prior to board consideration. If the Directors certify that the project meets appropriate engineering, environmental and financial standards, the Commission will try to assemble a financing package from private, public and international sources.

j)   *The North American Development Bank*

There are a number of sources that might go towards meeting the estimated US$6 to US$8 billion financing needs for environmental infrastructure along the border. Private sources will play an important role to the extent that increased economic activity can attract these resources. In addition, state and local development program funds will be available on the US side of the border, and funding from the World Bank and the Inter-American Development Bank will be available on the Mexican side. These resources might account from one-half to two thirds of all the financing needed. The remainder will be made up by the NADBank. The NADBank will be capitalised and governed by both the United States and Mexico. Its purpose is to finance projects certified by the Border Environment Co-operation Commission, and to provide support for NAFTA-related community adjustment and investment on both sides of the border. The Bank's capital shares (US$450 million of paid-in capital and US$2.55 billion of callable capital) will be contributed equally by the United States and Mexico. It is expected that the Bank will be able to make between US$2 and US$3 billion of loans or loan guarantees for projects related to border environmental infrastructure.

The NADBank has a six-member board of directors, composed of three cabinet level officials each from the United States and Mexico. It is located in San Antonio. Ten per cent of the resources of the Bank have been made available, on an equal basis, for community adjustment and investment in both countries related to the effects of NAFTA. This is not limited to the Border region. The community adjustment and investment financing on the US side will be funnelled through existing government sponsored credit programmes targeting special help for those US communities particularly affected by NAFTA. On the Mexican side the funds will be administered by Mexican development banks.

D. *Implementation of the Agreement*

Twelve months after the Agreement went into effect, the five principal institutions are operating and are in the process of getting organised. The Free Trade Secretariat which is the main administrative body of the Agreement is situated in Mexico City. The Environmental Co-operation Commission is situated in Montreal, Canada and a Mexican national has been named as director. The Labour Co-operation Commission is situated in Dallas, Texas. The Border Environmental Co-operation Commission established in Cuidad Juárez, Chihuahua, Mexico. Finally, the NADBank has been established in San Antonio, Texas.

In the matter of dispute resolution there have been a number of demands brought on both sides under the Agreement on Labour Co-operation. The first two of these demands were petitions brought by unions in the United States to the National Administrative Offices of the Labour Co-operation Commission regarding the laying off of Mexican workers in two Maquiladora plants along the Mexico-US border (Honeywell and General Electric). The

US unions alleged that the workers were laid off because they were attempting to create an independent union, and that the action interfered with their rights to organise and to have freedom of association. The National Administrative Office took the case under review, and ruled on 13 October 1994 that there was not sufficient evidence in the case to move the dispute to ministerial review, and that Mexican authorities had not failed to enforce their own labour laws. The National Administrative Office in the United States is also reviewing two more petitions from four US groups, among them the International Labour Rights Education and Research Fund (ILRERF), against a Sony plant in Nuevo Laredo and a General Electric plant in Ciudad Juárez, for similar allegations.

There have also been petitions on the side of Mexico. The National Telephone Workers Union has brought a petition against the National Administrative Office in Mexico against a subsidiary of Sprint for violating US labour laws. The petition alleges that the company laid off 235 workers that were attempting to form an independent union. In addition, it alleges that the petition for reinstatement of the workers was unjustly thrown out by US arbitration panels.

In addition to labour disputes, there have been a number of anti-dumping complaints brought by the parties of NAFTA. The first dispute was in the case of countervailing duties placed by Mexico on imports of certain types of steel imports from the United States. A panel was convened under the dispute settlement procedures of NAFTA in November 1994. So far, there have been four disputes brought by Mexican exporters questioning the legality of US imposed countervailing duties on imports of leather wear, porcelain-on-steel cookware, cement and oil tubes from Mexico.

More recently (May 1995) there was a complaint brought by the US Trade Representative to Mexican authorities about a breach of the national treatment provisions of NAFTA in the express-delivery business. US express-delivery companies such as United Parcel Service, Federal Express and Airborne Freight have complained that the Mexican Government has denied them licenses to use large trucks to deliver their packages and letters within Mexico. Mexican firms require no such licenses and can use large trucks to deliver their shipments. Under the provisions of NAFTA dispute settlement procedures there is a period of 30 days in which the parties have a chance to solve the dispute. After this period, if there is no resolution then the issue will go to arbitration. This is the first dispute over national treatment brought under the NAFTA.

E.   *Results after the first year of implementation*

a)   Trade

Bilateral trade and investment flows between the United States and Mexico and between Canada and Mexico grew considerably in the first year of the implementation of the Agreement. According to the Bank of Mexico (Banxico), for 1994 the value of trade between the United States and Mexico was US$106.4 billion, an increase of 20.7 per cent over the previous year. Mexican exports to the United States increased by 24.1 per cent while US exports to Mexico increased by 20.5 per cent. Mexico's balance of trade with the United States remained negative, but fell by 28.7 per cent. Mexico's trade with Canada also increased by 13.1 per cent, although it started from a low base in 1993 of US$2 744 million. Mexico's exports to Canada showed a deficit of 5.5 per cent, while Canadian exports to Mexico increased by 38 per cent.

Manufactured and semi-manufactured commodities made up the largest increase in trade during 1994, especially iron and steel, speedometers and tachometers, computers, sweaters and jerseys, gasoline combustion engines, finished automobiles, stoves, refrigerators, telephonic equipment, air pumps and compressors, and textiles in general.

b)   Investment

In 1994, FDI from the United States and Canada continued to flow to Mexico. US investment amounted to US$4 004 million, 49.9 per cent of the total of foreign investment flow during the year, and up 14.3 per cent from the previous year. Canadian investment amounted to US$162.5 million, or 5 per cent of the total yearly flow and up 120 per cent over the previous year. Much of this investment came in the form of joint ventures between US, Canadian and Mexican businessmen. More than 500 joint ventures were established in 1994, of which the most important were: Cifra-Walmart, Comercial Mexicana-Price Costco, Gigante-Fleming, Liverpool-K-Mart, Sara Lee-Axa Alimentos, Crystal Brand-Suéteres de Alta Tecnología, Grupo Femsa-Labatt, and Altos Hornos-Inland Steel. In financial services, the expected opening of the Mexican market under NAFTA has brought over 102 applications for investment in the financial sector, with an approximate value of US$1.5 billion.

c)   *Employment*

According to the US Department of Labour, during 1994 the programme for Trade Adjustment Assistance under NAFTA benefited 17 000 workers, including those from Nintendo of America, Emerson Electric, Northern Telecom, Key Tronic, Johnson Controls, Eaton Corporation, USA Enterprises, Pope & Talbott and Waynesboro Apparel. The Trade Adjustment Assistance programme grants workers aid equivalent to the amount they received from unemployment insurance in their state after their eligibility for unemployment insurance runs out. The aid continues for 52 weeks after regular unemployment insurance finishes, on the condition that workers enrol in special worker retraining programmes. The programme is designed to aid workers directly or indirectly affected by plant closings related to NAFTA.

2.   Other regional trade agreements

The fact that the NAFTA accession clause has not yet been tested has made it unclear from the start whether this mechanism would result in an eventual free trade area across the continent as envisioned in the Enterprise for the Americas Initiative of the Bush administration. To date the only country that has petitioned for NAFTA accession has been Chile. The Government of Chile formally presented its petition for NAFTA accession at the Summit of the Americas meetings in Miami in December of 1994, which concentrated on trade issues. The process of accession is complicated by the fact that the negotiation of accession terms must be authorised by the US Congress, which has up to this point been reluctant to grant fast track negotiating authority to the US Trade Representative[7].

Mexico made the decision to pursue bilateral free trade agreements with other countries in Latin America. These initiatives are part of a broader policy of support to the multilateral trading institutions and the pursuit of individual (bilateral) opportunities to ensure access to markets in Latin America. To date Mexico has signed free trade agreements with Chile (September 1991), Costa Rica (April 1994), Colombia and Venezuela (June 1994) and Bolivia (September 1994). At the time of this writing there were also negotiations in process or planned with Nicaragua, the Northern Cone of Central America (Guatemala, Honduras and El Salvador) and with the EU. The free trade agreement with Chile is actually a broader "Economic Complementarity Accord" which differs in some respects from the NAFTA and subsequent trade agreements. The Accord with Chile and the differences between it and NAFTA are reviewed below. Subsequent free trade agreements follow the pattern of the NAFTA very closely, with differences in sector emphasis according to the composition of trade between Mexico and its partner.

A. *Mexico-Chile Economic Complementarity Accord*

The Mexico-Chile Economic Complementarity Accord (ACE)[8] came into force on 1 January 1992. It predates NAFTA and thus can be seen as the first of the major free trade initiatives pursued by Mexico in the last five years. The first part of the Accord contains a programme of bilateral trade liberalisation that will end in the establishment of a free trade zone between the two countries. The second part presents the rules under which liberalisation will take place, including rules of origin, safeguards, dispute settlement, unfair trade practices (including anti-dumping), domestic tax treatment, air and sea transport, and trade promotion. Finally, the Accord addresses trade related economic issues such as investment, government procurement, services, technical standards and economic co-operation.

The ACE covers much of the same ground that was subsequently covered in the NAFTA, and contains very similar provisions on unfair trade practices and dispute settlement mechanisms. But there are some crucial differences. Unlike NAFTA, the language in the ACE does not invoke the general principles of market access, national treatment or MFN treatment. It only provides specifically for a reduction of tariffs and elimination of non-tariff barriers for particular products traded between the two countries. In this respect, when the Accord went into effect the maximum tariff allowed between the two countries was 10 per cent. This tariff would be reduced over a period of five years for the majority of products, and six years for a small subset including some agricultural, chemical and petrochemical, forestry, textile and glass products. Only a small number of products, including petroleum and derivatives, some marine products, some agricultural products, vegetable oils, powdered milk and used clothing, were excluded from the tariff reductions in the Accord. The Accord also has specific provisions for the automobile sector: reduction of all tariffs and non-tariff barriers on 1 January 1996, with rules of origin establishing a minimum of 32 per cent national content, and an annual quota allowing exports of automobiles with 16 per cent national content.

The ACE also differs from NAFTA in the following provisions:

– The rules of origin provisions are not based on a change in tariff classification to confer origin, but rather on a 50 per cent or greater national value added rule.

– The treatment of services is another area where NAFTA invokes general principles of national and MFN treatment, while the ACE has specific sector provisions. The ACE only refers explicitly to maritime and commercial air transportation. In maritime transportation there is a provision for open access to maritime cargo by ships running the flag of either country (i.e. national treatment). In commercial air transport, the Accord allows the establishment of commercial routes (regular or non-regular) between Mexico City and Santiago de Chile, and any other destination in between. For other services, the Accord states that the parties will promote measures to liberalise service trade in line with what was established under the General Agreement on Trade in Services (GATS). This is in contrast to NAFTA which explicitly excludes most maritime and commercial air transport, but which establishes principles and rules for increased trade in other services. In addition, the ACE does not have provisions for the temporary entry of business persons.

– The ACE goes beyond NAFTA in other areas, such as the agreement to establish joint programmes for trade promotion and business integration between the two countries, and the agreement to pursue economic co-operation on trade policy, financial, monetary and tax policy, and transfer of technology.

– In the area of technical standards, the ACE sets up a review mechanism (under the Commission that will administer the Accord) that will analyse technical standards and recommend solutions where these are found to obstruct trade. This is a much broader and vaguer statute than that pursued under NAFTA, which includes specific trade disciplines related to technical standards, including national or MFN treatment with respect to standards.

– In the area of investment, the ACE does specify that each country will extend the more favourable of national or MFN treatment to the other. However, it lacks the broad definition of investment included in NAFTA (which includes issues of intellectual property rights, capital movements and other kinds of resource transfers). In addition, it does not include the provisions guaranteeing free convertibility and transfer of capital or indemnisation in the case of expropriation. The ACE also does not include provisions against trade-related investment measures or trade-related intellectual property violations.

– Government procurement in the ACE is governed by reciprocity and GATT consistent rules. In NAFTA there are provisions for national treatment, transparency of bidding procedures and minimum values of contracts subject to bids by signatories.

In addition to the above, there are some provisions in NAFTA that were not included in the ACE. The most important of these is the provision on intellectual property rights (IPRs). In NAFTA there is a separate chapter dealing with IPRs in which the parties are guaranteed national and MFN treatment with respect to all intellectual property rights issues, trademark protection, copyright guarantees, and the protection of industrial secrets. The ACE also has no formal accession clause, and no mention of internal institutions to enforce domestic competition policy.

B.   *Other Free Trade Agreements*

By definition, regional trade agreements create "insiders" and "outsiders", and the debate about whether these agreements are desirable centres on the question of discrimination. One element of this issue is the dichotomy between trade creation and trade diversion. The more inward-looking and protectionist regional agreements are *vis-à-vis* third countries, the more likely it is that trade diversion will swamp trade creation. On the other hand, agreements that are open, where preferential margins tend to be low, are far more likely to create positive effects for their members and for outsiders *via* additional trading opportunities. Where several different agreements co-exist, such as in the case of Mexico's network of regional agreements, it may become increasingly difficult to ensure that trade distortions do not enter the picture. Even where it is the intention of a government to guard against the emergence of such distortions, the sheer complexity of overlapping agreements may create inadvertent inconsistencies and economic costs.

A second issue arising with multiple overlapping regional agreements relates to administrative costs to the extent that there are differences. The administrative authorities responsible for customs, rules of origin, standards, and a range of other trade-related policy matters are required to administer different sets of rules and procedures in a coherent manner. Otherwise, the mere existence of a multiplicity of agreements can constitute barriers to trade.

In sum, trade distortions will be kept to a minimum if governments refrain from using regional agreements as protectionist havens, such that non-preferential barriers to trade, or in other words, the trade regime faced by third countries, is not too restrictive. Administrative obstacles will also be minimised if different regional agreements not too dissimilar. Indeed, if regional initiatives are designed to open up trading opportunities rather than close out third parties, there is no reason why different regional agreements in which a country like Mexico is involved will not be similar in design and content. By extension, there should be no obstacle, in principle, to the gradual fusion of separate regional agreements into a coherent whole.

A question to consider, is how far Mexico's newer FTAs with other Latin American countries conform with NAFTA, which represents the single most important regime for Mexican trade, at least in terms of current trade flows. An examination of these agreements suggests a high degree of uniformity, certainly in terms of the approach to core commitments, and also for the most part in relation to more detailed commitments. Some exceptions naturally occur, such as the exclusion from national treatment of textiles in the case of Venezuela, and of polystyrene in the case of both Venezuela and Colombia, in the context of the G-3 agreement. Variations also commonly occur in the time frames set for full compliance with certain obligations, but this is relatively unimportant, given the prior commitment that exists for full convergence over time.

As regards product-level specificity, or non-uniformity, all the agreements contain special, sui generis provisions on agriculture, but all within a context of continuing trade liberalisation. The situation is similar with respect to motor vehicles.

The design of the rules of origin is very similar to NAFTA in all the recent FTAs. They specify that goods will qualify for origin if they are made in their totality from national inputs, have experienced a significant transformation in the region which is evidenced by a change in tariff classification, or have a given level of regional value. Regional content is measured as a percentage of the transaction value of the good and the level varies from 40 to 50 per cent for most products. For the FTA with Bolivia, the net cost valuation for domestic content is permitted with a minimum level of 41.6 per cent. Special treatment is given to a number of products, including chemicals and plastics, textiles, steel, copper and aluminium. In some cases (Mexico-Bolivia) a longer transition period is provided before rules of origin come into effect. In others (Mexico-G3 and Mexico-Costa Rica), special committees are set up to evaluate the capacity of each country to supply domestic inputs to these industries as a basis for future configuration of rules of origin.

The safeguard provisions are identical for the FTAs and NAFTA. They establish the possibility of applying temporary bilateral tariff measures to protect a national industry against damaging increases in imports as a result of the reduction of tariffs under the agreement. These safeguards must be price based, and may last no longer than two years. In addition, there is a compensation mechanism in the case that these safeguards are used for unjustified protection. Finally, each party reserves the right to adopt emergency safeguard measures under the WTO Safeguards Agreement. It is interesting to note, however, that the safeguards mechanisms included in the FTAs are significantly stricter than the WTO provisions, particularly in relation to the injunction against the use of non-tariff barriers as safeguard measures, and in terms of the time frame for action.

The sections of the agreements dealing with anti-dumping and subsidies and countervailing duties also follow the NAFTA model closely. A commitment is established by parties to eliminate all subsidies to bilateral exports, and the right is established to levy countervailing duties on imported goods that have received subsidies or anti-dumping duties where goods are found to be subsidised or dumped and to have caused injury to domestic industry.

Similar to NAFTA, investment rules under the other FTAs establish a broad definition of investment, which includes most types of resource transfers and is "congruent with other trade agreements subscribed to by Mexico". The basic principles applied are non-discriminatory national or MFN treatment, freedom of transfer of resources and full indemnisation in the case of expropriation. In addition, the imposition of performance standards for investment such as trade-related investment measures or trade-related intellectual property restrictions are prohibited.

These few examples illustrate the likeness between NAFTA and more recent FTAs in which Mexico is involved. Similar points could have been made in such diverse areas as trade in services, procurement, standards, intellectual property rights, and dispute settlement. Finally, an accession clause leaves the possibility of other countries joining these accords subject to the terms and conditions that the signatories may impose. Stated in this manner, the accession clauses suggest an open-ended approach to the possibility of including new signatories to existing FTAs.

NOTES

1   For a comprehensive bibliography of NAFTA related studies see Manuel Pastor Jr., "Mexican Trade Liberalization and NAFTA" *Latin American Research Review*.

2   This section relies extensively on previous summaries of the Agreement, particularly Hufbauer and Schott (1993), "NAFTA An Assessment, Institute for International Economics", Washington D.C., Feb. 1993, and "Government's of Canada, The United Mexican States and The United States of America" (1992).

3   These include petroleum exploration, extraction and refining, as well as gasoline sales.

4   If the regulations are at the state or province level then the national treatment provisions require treatment no less favourable than that given to a local state or province provider.

5   In this respect the Mexican and the US systems are quite different. Professional certification in Mexico is a centralised Government function that is administered through the Ministry of Education. In the United States, most professions are self regulated through mechanisms like state bar exams or medical certification exams.

6   "Government's of Canada, The United Mexican States and The United States of America", (1992), p. 20.

7   Fast track authority allows the US executive to negotiate a trade agreement and bring it to the congress for a vote of approval within 90 days of the presentation of the trade bill without the addition of amendments or changes, thus avoiding what could be very lengthy negotiations inside Congress on the merits of the agreement and implications for changes.

8   *Acuerdo de Complementación Económica Mexico-Chile.*

CHAPTER 5

MEXICO IN THE URUGUAY ROUND

Mexico was an active participant in the Uruguay Round negotiations - a reflection of its concern with multilateralism, not just regionalism. This chapter looks at the main results of the Round, in terms of market access commitments by Mexico, and examines the significance for Mexico of changes in the rules area. A central question is: will Mexico have to undertake significant policy reform as a result of the Uruguay Round or did the results primarily consolidate the *status quo*?

1. The Uruguay Round and the multilateral trading system

As Herminio Blanco, Mexico's Minister of International Trade, stated in January 1994 at the conclusion of the negotiations, "Mexico is an important beneficiary of these negotiations, but it has also contributed significantly to their success"[1]. In the area of tariff negotiations, Mexico applied a linear reduction from 50 to 35 per cent *ad valorem* with some exceptions, but its trade partners would have preferred to see a greater reduction in its bound tariff rates which generally remain higher than its applied rates. In agriculture, notwithstanding its legal rights under its Protocol of accession to the GATT, Mexico joint other countries with some reluctance in the tariffication of all its non-tariff barriers including certain very "sensitive" products such as maize, kidney beans and dairy products. While it received somewhat improved access to its export markets, it was disappointed that more significant reductions were not stipulated for domestic support and that export subsidies in agriculture were not eliminated. In the area of trade rules, despite its export oriented position the moderate increase in disciplines on anti-dumping actions suited its dual status: Mexico is subject to such actions in its export markets and itself initiates such actions against imports. With regard to subsidies, Mexico's proposal, that certain subsidies for the purposes of environmental protection should not be countervailable, was endorsed. In the context of dispute settlement, Mexico promoted greater certainty through the establishment of time limits and the introduction of the quasi-automaticity for the adoption of panel reports. It also supported the maintenance of special and differential treatment for developing countries, primarily with regard to certain procedural issues. On institutional issues, Mexico was the first participant to submit, together with Canada and the United States, a concrete proposal to establish the WTO. However, on the whole, the Minister's verdict on the services negotiations, that "the results are undoubtedly satisfactory, but we did not take advantage of the opportunity to make greater progress in sectors of prime importance worldwide", is probably valid even outside the services context.

2. Mexico's own trade policy reforms

As discussed in earlier chapters, since late 1984 Mexico has initiated significant economic reforms which have included trade liberalisation, privatisation and deregulation. The reforms have transformed Mexico from an inward-looking economy, with heavy government intervention, into a largely open economy reliant on private enterprise.

Non-tariff restrictions on imports, such as import licenses, have been largely eliminated. In 1993, less than 2 per cent of tariff lines were subject to import licensing compared to 100 per cent in 1982. The goods still subject to import licensing, *via* prior import permits, included principally agricultural goods, as well as petroleum and petroleum products, arms and ammunition, certain automobiles, and, on a temporary basis, pharmaceutical products. Table 20 shows the type of non-tariff measures imposed by Latin American countries[2]. Mexico, along with Brazil, stands out due to the presence of state monopolies and non-automatic licensing, which includes local content regulations and export-performance requirements in the UNCTAD classification.

Mexico has substantially reduced and rationalised its tariffs. As part of its accession to the GATT in 1986, Mexico was the first acceding country which has agreed to bind its entire tariff schedule, including agricultural and industrial products, generally at a level of 50 per cent *ad valorem* (with some exceptions at a lower rate). There is, however, a considerable gap between currently applied and bound rates. Applied rates range from zero to 20 per cent, with a simple average of 13 per cent in 1992, compared to 22.6 per cent in 1986 and 27 per cent in 1982[3]. The trade weighted average also fell from 16.4 per cent in 1982 to 13.1 per cent in 1986 and around 10 per cent in 1992.

Mexico has also reduced the coverage of, and variation in, its export taxes. In 1992, taxes were levied on 24 of the 5 183 export items (at the 6-digit HS level): 20 items were taxed at 50 per cent and four at 25 per cent. The present structure compares favourably with the one in the early 1980s; for example, in 1983, there were 16 different rates levied on 173 export items. The products affected by export taxes are certain live animals, certain petroleum derivatives, human blood, and certain goods considered to be of historical importance.

3.   Main market access results

A.   *Tariffs and non-tariff measures*

Table 21 shows industrial country tariff reductions in a range of industrial product categories resulting from the Uruguay Round. The percentage reduction in weighted tariff averages on different categories of industrial goods varies between 19 and 69 per cent in relation to developing countries imports, making an average of 37 per cent for all industrial products. This rate of reduction can be compared to the 40 per cent weighted average reduction in respect of industrial country imports from all sources.

Table 22 indicates the improvements made in binding levels in the Uruguay Round. In developed countries, bindings on industrial products are near 100 per cent, as they are in transition economies. The most dramatic change is in developing countries, where bindings increased from 21 to 73 per cent in terms of tariff lines, and from 13 to 61 per cent in terms of import coverage. In agriculture, all countries were required to bind all their tariffs, but again, the change was most dramatic in the case of developing countries.

Table 23 provides information on pre- and post-Uruguay Round liberalisation in different regions, taking into account both tariffs and non-tariff barriers. According to the Table, Latin American levels of protection in non-agricultural sectors remain higher on average than those prevailing in any other region except South Asia. The weighted average protection level, measured as a composite of tariffs and the tariff equivalents of non-tariff measures, was 24 per cent in Latin America before the Uruguay Round and will be 18 per cent by the time the liberalisation has been fully phased in.

As noted above, as part of its accession to the GATT in 1986, Mexico had already bound its entire tariff schedule, including agricultural and industrial products. Bindings were made at ceiling levels, and subsequently applied tariff rates have become significantly lower than bound rates. The lower applied rates represent accumulated unilateral liberalisation undertaken by Mexico over the last few years. Mexico undertook a significant reduction in its bound rates during the Uruguay Round, from an ceiling level of about 50 to 35 per cent *ad valorem* for non-agricultural products (with certain exceptions).

The import-weighted average applied and bound rates are shown in Table 24. It is evident that even though there were significant declines in bound rates in all product categories, yielding a trade-weighted average of some 40 per cent, bound rates remained above applied rates in most cases, and often by a large margin. The reduction in bound rates is, nevertheless, still a move towards trade liberalisation since it has the effect of reducing the level to which the national government could increase the tariff in the future. This reduction in the range of potential tariff increases has the effect of reducing the expected tariff level and its variance -- thus reducing the expected levels of protection and the uncertainty that exporters and investors face[4]. Even though tariff bindings above applied rates have intrinsic worth, there is some concern because rates can be increased more easily than if they were applied at bound rates. It may be argued that maintenance of a large gap between bound and applied rates means that a country is not fully committed to its current level of liberalism in trade policy. On the other hand, it may also be argued that this gap exists because GATT does not provide incentive to take duly account of unilateral liberalisation measures. Mexico submitted a proposal during the Uruguay Round to provide "credit" for bindings and "recognition" for unilateral liberalisation measures. In its opinion, finding a way to recognise unilateral liberalisation measures within the WTO will promote further liberalisation by developing countries while at the same time providing some certainty to their partners. This complex issue is under the terms of reference of the WTO Committee on Trade and Development for further discussion.

B.   *Agricultural negotiations*

Under the Agreement on Agriculture, countries committed themselves to reduce trade-distorting domestic subsidies, to freeze and reduce export subsidies, and to convert all non-tariff measures affecting imports into tariffs and subject these tariffs to staged reductions. Mexico was an active participant in the agricultural negotiations. Its objectives included, among others, obtaining improved access for its key exports (tropical products and fruits and vegetables), in order to generate the necessary income to compensate possible price increases (due to the elimination or reduction of subsidies) on its imports of agricultural commodities. On market access Mexico sought to exclude from tariffication some very sensitive products (maize, kidney beans and dairy products) but at the end it agreed to tariffy all products under the general rules of tariffication. On subsidies, Mexico was keen to see the total elimination of export subsidies and when it was clear that such elimination would not be acceptable by other countries or group of countries, it proposed that the developing countries should be permitted to "match" other countries export subsidies on a case by case basis, in order to defend their exports in third markets. In Mexico's perception, universal tariffication was a significant achievement of the negotiations, but the solution reached to the problem of reduction of internal subsidies and export subsidies was only preliminary and incomplete.

a)   *Domestic support measures*

Commitments on reductions in domestic support levels are expressed in terms of a "Total Aggregate Measure of Support," (Total AMS) which is defined as the sum of all domestic support measures provided in favour of agricultural producers which are deemed to be more than minimally production and trade distorting. Industrial countries are committed to an average reduction of 20 per cent in respect of their Total AMS calculated for 1986-88 over a six-year period. The commitment made by developing countries, including Mexico, is for 13.3 per cent over ten years. Note that domestic support reduction commitments are to be implemented in terms of "Annual and Final Bound Commitment Levels," and that they are not product specific. Mexico declared base Total AMS of around 29 billion pesos in 1991, scheduled to be reduced between 1995 and 2004 to a little over 25 billion pesos.

Until the mid-80s, government support to the agricultural sector in Mexico was channelled primarily through purchases from producers of basic commodities (grains and oilseeds) at guaranteed prices, while keeping input prices and prices to consumers low through subsidies[5]. In 1993, the Mexican government introduced a new income support programme (Programme of Direct Payments to the Countryside) giving farmers twice yearly fixed acreage payments to progressively replace the system of price support to grains and oilseeds producers. Increasingly, subsidies for basic foods (tortillas, beans and milk) have been targeted towards the poorest or most needy groups in the population. Since 1990, substantial reforms have been introduced in rural credit policy resulting in reduced interest concessions in agriculture. In 1992, FERTIMEX (Mexican Fertilizer Company) was privatised and fertilizer subsidies were terminated. A new Water Law was passed in 1992 to decentralise the management of irrigation districts to improve incentives for operation and maintenance cost recovery.

While subsidies and direct income transfers mentioned above are in line with Mexico's commitments on domestic support reductions in the WTO, it should nevertheless be borne in mind that such measures carry significant budgetary implications.

b)   *Export subsidy commitments*

The Agreement imposes a freeze on all export subsidy levels measured from a 1986-90 base, and requires an average reduction of 36 per cent in the value of subsidies and 21 per cent in the volume of subsidised exports over a period of six years. Lower percentage reductions over a ten-year period are required from developing countries. Even though Mexico did not grant export subsidies, it declared certain amounts of export subsidies in the base period for five products (maize, beans, wheat, sorghum and sugar) in order to retain the flexibility to grant such subsidies in future up to the levels permitted by the Agreement. Disposing excess domestic production over consumption with export subsidies can be economically costly and it is hoped that Mexico will refrain from using export subsidies.

c)   *Tariffs and non-tariff measures*

As already noted, the Agreement requires that all non-tariff measures are converted into tariffs, expressed either in *ad valorem* or specific terms. In addition, all these tariffs are to be bound in countries' schedules of commitments. The decision to require the binding of all tariffs was novel, since this has not yet been achieved in the area of manufactures. Prior to the universal binding in agriculture, some 81 per cent of industrial country imports from this sector entered under bound tariff lines, while the relevant figures for developing countries and countries in transition were 22 and 59 per cent respectively. No new non-tariff measures may be adopted, unless they can be justified under other WTO provisions (e.g. balance-of-payments problems or safeguards).

The Agreement defines non-tariff measures as quantitative restrictions, minimum import prices, discretionary import licensing regimes, non-tariff measures applied through state-trading enterprises, voluntary export restraints, and similar border measures other than ordinary customs duties. The base year for tariffication is 1986-88.

Nominal tariffs are to be reduced by at least 15 per cent on all products, and by an average of 36 per cent overall. The reductions are to take place over a six-year period. For developing countries, including Mexico, the commitment is for a minimum 10 per cent reduction on all products and an average of 24 per cent, over a period of ten years. Tariff quotas are to be applied to ensure market access levels in line with previous import levels. Where no previous imports existed, minimum access commitments have been established. Despite its initial reluctance in the case of some products, Mexico eventually complied with these requirements. Preliminary estimates suggest that tariffs in the agricultural sector are likely to decline from an import-weighted base level of 77 per cent to an eventual import-weighted bound level of 67 per cent once all the cuts have been made (Table 24).

C.   Textiles and clothing sector

The Agreement on Textiles and Clothing stipulates that products covered under the Multifibre Arrangement (MFA) will be reintegrated into mainstream WTO disciplines over a period of ten years, in four different stages. Tariffs on textiles and clothing products applied by the major industrial country importers will only be reduced by a weighted average of 22 per cent under the Uruguay Round tariff commitments, resulting in an average level of protection of 12 per cent[6]. The depth of this cut compares unfavourably with the overall weighted average of around 40 per cent, and the resulting level is still more than three times the average level on all manufactured products. As quotas are reduced, these tariffs will become relatively more important as instruments of protection.

The limited reduction in textile tariffs is of concern to Mexico, since its exports are subject to quantitative restrictions only in the United States for non-originating goods under NAFTA, in 14 categories. These restrictions, originally under the MFA but now under NAFTA, are scheduled to be eliminated for ten categories by the year 2001 and for the rest by the year 2004. Textile products covered by the Agreement are those made from cotton and wool fibres as well as from artificial and synthetic fibres, classified in

133 categories under four groups (yarns, fabrics, garment and other textile manufactures).

4. Non-tariff measures in the Uruguay Round

A. *Safeguards*

The safeguard provisions allow governments to impose tariffs or quantitative restrictions on imports for a limited time period if the imports in question are growing in such a fashion as to cause or threaten to cause serious injury to a domestic industry. The contents of the Safeguards Agreement reflect an attempt to rectify the fact that the GATT safeguards provisions have fallen into virtual disuse in recent years as governments have chosen less transparent instruments to grant industry-specific protection.

Actions against imports aimed at providing relief to import-competing domestic industries have relied increasingly on "grey area measures" such as voluntary export restraints and anti-dumping and countervailing duty actions. The lack of transparency of voluntary export restraints, their essentially discriminatory nature, and the role played by exporting countries in their application, have made them more attractive than safeguards.

Mexican exports are not subject to safeguard actions under GATT or to grey area measures. Mexican legislation on safeguard measures was previously made up of various provisions of the Mexican Foreign Trade Act and its Regulations, and now has been supplemented by the Agreement on Safeguards. The Foreign Trade Act provides for the restriction or regulation of imports when increases in their volume cause or threaten to cause serious injury to domestic producers. In the Report of the Working Party on the Accession of Mexico to GATT, the Mexican Delegation noted that in taking safeguard measures, Mexico would abide by the provisions of Article XIX of the GATT[7].

The new safeguards Agreement to an extent fulfilled Mexico's objectives of introducing stricter disciplines on safeguards and special and differential treatment for developing countries. Mexico was initially opposed to the possibility of discriminatory safeguard action, but eventually accepted the possibility of quota modulation.

B.   Anti-dumping and countervailing duties

Efforts to introduce greater discipline in the use of these measures in the Uruguay Round met with only partial success. Some improvements were made to the methodological requirements for calculating dumping margins and determining injury. Clearer definitions were established of what constitutes a domestic industry (the proportion of the industry required to attain standing), and a number of requirements relating to investigation procedures and standards of evidence were more fully specified. Certain *de minimis* thresholds were introduced, below which actions are to be automatically discontinued. A "sunset" provision was established, requiring that anti-dumping and countervailing duty measures remain in place no longer than five years, unless a review demonstrates that the removal of the measure would lead to a recurrence of the original problem.

It would be fair to say that Mexico wanted strict disciplines on anti-dumping actions because such measures have been used both by others against its exports and by Mexico itself against imports. Among WTO members, Mexico is one of the most frequent user of anti-dumping actions. Between 1985/86 and 1993/94, Mexico had initiated 131 anti-dumping investigations against GATT members, while 25 investigations had been initiated against its exports. The exports which have been affected include those of cement, iron and steel, cut flowers, synthetic and acrylic fibres, and sisal twine. In the case of cement, Mexico requested the creation of a panel in the Anti-Dumping Committee, which found in favour of Mexico. Mexico views with concern the growing number of new users who in some cases have unjustifiably resorted to the use of anti-dumping measures[8].

Mexico changed its anti-dumping legislation to bring it in line with its obligations under NAFTA. Changes to the Mexican anti-dumping legislation are underway to make it compatible with WTO obligations.

C.   Subsidies

Some progress was made in the Uruguay Round in establishing tighter disciplines on the use of subsidies. Subsidies were defined for the first time. The definition includes financial contributions or transfers by governments, foregone revenue to the benefit of enterprises, the provision of goods or services (free or at less than market price) other than infrastructure, and price supports from which producers benefit.

Subsidies are also classified in terms of three categories -- prohibited subsidies, actionable subsidies, and non-actionable subsidies. Prohibited subsidies include export subsidies on manufactured goods and subsidies contingent on the use of domestic rather than imported goods in production. Agricultural subsidies are not covered in this Agreement. Actionable subsidies are defined as those which are permissible, but which may attract countervailing or other action if they cause injury to domestic producer interests, nullification or impairment of benefits, or serious prejudice to the interest of another WTO member. Non-actionable subsidies include non-specific subsidies, assistance for certain research activities, regional subsidies, and subsidies for the environmental adaptation of plant and machinery.

In the negotiations, Mexico was keen to obtain non-actionable status under both multilateral disciplines and national rules for certain environmental subsidies, including those for environment-related research and development. Furthermore, Mexico sought a similar status for certain regional subsidies which it uses to shift economic activity away from Mexico city and other large centres. In these objectives it was largely successful, since, as indicated above, it was agreed that both these types of subsidies should be non-actionable. Mexico also received satisfaction on its proposal to give a "credit" to those developing countries which would phase out their export subsidies ahead of the scheduled time limit of eight years.

D.   *Balance-of-payments measures*

Article XVIII:B of GATT 1994 allows developing countries to maintain import restrictions on a temporary basis in order to deal with a foreign exchange shortage (Article XII is a stricter, and rarely used, version of these provisions meant for industrial countries). The Uruguay Round Understanding on this subject seeks to strengthen these disciplines, in order to control the practice of using the balance-of-payments provisions as a means of providing protection to particular industries. A basic principle of these rules is that they should apply to a wide range of imports, and not be targeted on particular sectors. At the same time, it is recognised that governments may wish to prioritise their restrictions in the light of how essential particular items in the import bill are considered to be.

Mexico has no import restrictions in place in order to deal with balance-of-payments problems and has never invoked Article XVIII:B of GATT. In response to the financial crisis of 1994, there was recourse primarily to macroeconomic rather than to trade policy instruments, in contrast to the 1982 balance-of-payments crisis, when import licensing was extended to cover all imports.

E.   *Technical barriers to trade*

The WTO rules on technical barriers to trade build on earlier rules drawn up in the Tokyo Round. They are designed to ensure that standards do not create any unnecessary barriers to trade, nor lead to unwarranted discrimination among trading partners. The Agreement tries to ensure that standards adopted are the least trade-restrictive possible, and establishes a code of good practice for the preparation, adoption, and application of standards.

The Agreement does not impose international standards, but encourages governments to adopt them, and emphasizes the advantages of harmonized standards and related procedures, including conformity assessment systems. The Agreement acknowledges, however, that governments may prefer to set their own standards. New guidelines are established for the creation of voluntary standards.

Mexico was a signatory to the Tokyo Round Agreement on Technical Barriers to Trade. In the Uruguay Round of negotiations it played a special role in ensuring that the coverage of the Agreement was extended only to production and processing methods.

F.   *Sanitary and phytosanitary measures*

Although similar in substance to standards in general, sanitary and phytosanitary measures were dealt with separately as part of the agriculture negotiation. The Agreement permits governments to maintain the levels of standards that they consider necessary for the protection of human, animal and plant life and health. Standards may be stricter than those recommended by international bodies, provided they are based on scientific principles and appropriate risk assessment criteria. When standards adopted nationally differ from international standards, and have a significant effect on trade, they must be notified to the WTO and may be subject to examination. The Agreement is based on the principles of harmonisation and equivalence. As harmonized standards are developed internationally, it is expected that these will tend to be consistent with the objectives of the WTO agreement. Where harmonization is not possible or appropriate, the objective should be, as far as practicable, to attain equivalence. Both this and the standards Agreement are important elements in the WTO system of rules, because standards can be turned to protectionist ends with disconcerting ease.

Under NAFTA, Mexico has taken on rights and obligations which largely resemble those contained in the Uruguay Round Agreement on the Application of Sanitary and Phytosanitary Measures, with additional rules applying to specific regional conditions[9]. It has also been claimed that Mexico's exports are frequently affected by sanitary and phytosanitary standards that "have no strictly scientific basis"[10]. Examples given include barriers against some agricultural products such as poultry meat, avocados, chili peppers, squashes and strawberries. The new rules should help to reduce these problems.

G.   *Rules of origin*

The Uruguay Round Agreement on Rules of Origin establishes disciplines in respect of rules used in non-preferential trade. These rules are required whenever a country has a reason for discriminating among sources of supply, other than as a result of the existence of a preferential trading arrangement. Typically, such rules are applied to enforce such measures as anti-dumping and countervailing duties, standards, or some other measure that is intrinsically selective in a geographical sense. The Agreement sets out a three year work programme aimed at harmonizing non-preferential rules of origin.

Mexico does not apply specific rules of origin to imports from MFN sources. For imports benefitting from preferential entry from Latin American countries, the rules of origin applied by Mexico are those established by the Latin American Integration Association (LAIA)[11]. Similarly, rules of origin under NAFTA are designed to ensure that only goods produced in the North American region benefit from preferential treatment.

H.   *Import licensing*

An import licensing code was developed in the Tokyo Round with the objective of minimising the use of licensing arrangements as an additional and independent mechanism for restricting imports. Licensing should only be a means to an end, and any restrictive intent should be articulated as an explicit policy. The Agreement distinguishes between automatic and non-automatic licensing, with the objective of ensuring that non-automatic licensing is carried out in a consistent and transparent manner.

The Uruguay Round Agreement strengthens these provisions by establishing greater clarity with respect to procedures, time-frames for announcements and decisions, and the obligation to publish the decisions and intentions of the authorities.

As noted above, Mexico still uses import licenses for a small proportion of its imports. According to the Mexican Government, the mechanism for granting import licenses was consistent with provisions in the GATT Import Licensing Code. Even though the US Trade Representative in its National Trade Estimate Report on Foreign Trade Barriers (1991) made reference to "non-transparent" administration, no complaints have been made against Mexican practices under the Import Licensing Code[12].

5. State-trading enterprises

The new Agreement develops a clearer working definition of state-trading enterprises for notification purposes, and makes provision for the review of notifications and counter-notifications. Eight state-trading companies operate in Mexico[13]. The most important of these is CONASUPO which has a monopoly in the importation of milk powder. In addition, most import licenses granted by SECOFI for the importation of maize and kidney beans are given to CONASUPO. The company also imports other foodstuffs such as sorghum and soyabean. Purchasing practices of CONASUPO, as well as of other state trading enterprises, have to comply with Mexican legislation especially with respect to non-discrimination among suppliers and the application of commercial criteria for trade transactions[14] -- which are also the essential disciplines contained in Article XVII of the GATT.

6. Customs unions and free trade areas

The Uruguay Round Agreements made some modifications to Article XXIV of the GATT on customs unions and free trade areas, which essentially require that such agreements should involve the liberalisation of substantially all trade between members and should not lead to an increase in trade barriers against non-members. In the new Agreement, a methodology was established for the evaluation of duties before and after the formation of a customs union. Clear criteria were also set out for the review of existing or enlarged regional agreements. It was specified that interim agreements should normally lead to full-fledged agreements within ten years. Finally, there was a clarification of procedures to be followed when tariff bindings are renegotiated.

These developments are of particular relevance to Mexico. It signed a free trade agreement with Chile in 1991 and NAFTA in 1993. So far in 1995, Mexico has signed free trade agreements with Colombia and Venezuela, Costa Rica, Bolivia and negotiations are well underway with Ecuador, El Salvador, Guatemala, Honduras, and Nicaragua.

During the negotiations on Article XXIV, Mexico successfully argued against the Australian proposal that the definition of "substantially all trade" should make it clear the exclusion of whole sectors from the liberalisation requirement is inconsistent with Article XXIV. Mexico's intention was to avoid prejudging its forthcoming NAFTA negotiations presumably in the belief that it may be necessary to exclude some sectors (e.g. the petroleum sector). The Mexican position was supported by the European Free Trade Association (EFTA) and the European Community, who were concerned about the agricultural sector. As a result, the Article XXIV text contains only a weak recognition, in the preamble, that the exclusion of any major sector diminishes the contribution of a regional agreement to the expansion of world trade. NAFTA is currently under examination under Article XXIV of GATT 1994 for trade in goods and GATS Article V for trade in services.

7.   Trade-related investment measures

The Agreement provides that all trade-related investment measures (TRIMs) inconsistent with the principle of national treatment (Article III) and with the prohibition of quantitative trade restrictions (Article XI) are to be notified within 90 days and eliminated. Industrial countries must eliminate the offending measures within two years, developing countries within five years, and least-developed countries within seven years. Extensions of the time period may be possible under certain circumstances for the developing country categories.

During the past three decades, Mexico relied on local content requirements as part of its import-substitution industrial development policy, but now almost all local content requirements have been eliminated. For example, in 1990, local content requirements affecting the electronic industry were phased out. Such requirements are, however, maintained in the automobile sector. The motor vehicle assembly industry for small cars (of a gross weight of less than 8 864 kg) is required to incorporate a minimum local content of 36 per cent of the final value added. Minimum local content for motor vehicles (trucks and buses) weighing more than 8 864 kg is 40 per cent. The objective of these requirements is to promote the use of parts and components produced by the domestic auto parts industry. These requirements, in so far as they are inconsistent with the WTO, will need to be eliminated in accordance with the TRIMs Agreement[15].

8. Trade-related intellectual property rights

The Agreement on trade-related intellectual property rights (TRIPs) is the most comprehensive agreement of its kind, reflecting the determination of a number of industrial countries to establish strong disciplines in this field. The essential characteristics of the TRIPs Agreement include substantive rules in key areas of intellectual property rights, commitments on domestically-based enforcement provisions, and an international dispute settlement mechanism based on the ultimate right to take retaliatory trade measures in the face of intellectual property right infringements. The property rights involved cover minimum standards in respect of copyright, trademarks, geographical indications, industrial designs, patents, lay-out designs of integrated circuits, and protection of undisclosed information. The commitments build on existing international agreements, including the Paris Convention, the Bern Convention and the Rome Convention.

Mexico was a signatory to the Paris Convention on the protection of industrial property rights, and the Rome Convention on the rights of authors and artists. In the context of the NAFTA negotiations, Mexico has already accepted standards of protection for intellectual property which closely resemble those in the TRIPs Agreement. The Law for the Promotion and Protection of Intellectual Property Rights, enacted in July 1991, provides legal protection for exclusive use of inventions and trademarks, and streamlines the process for licensing of patents and trademarks. Mexico has already introduced unlimited pipeline protection. The NAFTA text substantially reproduces TRIPs provisions on matters such as compulsory licensing and anti-competitive practices, which were both areas of concern for Mexico. Mexico also had a particular interest in the protection of geographical indications for spirits, notably Mezcal and Tequila.

9.   Trade in services

The General Agreement on Trade in Services (GATS) extends multilateral rules to a broad range of service activities. The GATS is based on the non-discrimination principle, although it also envisages controlled departures from this rule. But these departures should in principle be eliminated within ten years. Some 70 countries have registered exceptions from the MFN requirement in various sectors. The GATS provides the necessary framework for establishing and maintaining liberalisation commitments, including through GATT-like provisions on transparency, regional agreements, general exceptions, security exceptions, and so on. Negotiations are to continue on provisions relating to safeguards, subsidies and government procurement.

Market access commitments are expressed in terms of four "modes of delivery" -- cross-border supply, cross-border movement of consumers to the jurisdiction of the producer, commercial presence, and cross-border movement of natural persons to the jurisdiction of the consumer. Commitments on these different modes depend on the nature of the service sector. For those services which cannot be delivered at arms-length, commercial presence or the temporary cross-border movement of producers or consumers are clearly a *sine qua non* of effective access. Unlike the GATT, national treatment is not a principle guaranteed *ex ante* (like the MFN or non-discrimination principle), but rather a negotiating objective, to be granted or denied on the basis of scheduled market access commitments.

Mexico undertook commitments in all sectors except environmental services and recreational, cultural and sporting services. Mexico's scheduled commitments are conditioned by a "horizontal" proviso limiting its commitments on the movement of natural persons, like most countries, to intra-corporate transferees at the executive and managerial levels and specialists. Restrictions on foreign ownership are the most frequently encountered limitation in the sector specific schedules. In numerous services, including professional services like accounting, auditing and bookkeeping services, certain telecommunication and audiovisual services, and all scheduled construction, private education and health services, there is a requirement that foreign investment must not exceed 49 per cent of the registered capital of enterprises.

In certain sectors, notably financial services, which exclude insurance services and are offered on the basis of commercial presence only, the limitations on foreign investment are more severe[16].. However, the limits on foreign ownership in commercial banks and securities houses were raised from 20 to 30 per cent as part of Mexico's improved offer in the extended negotiations on financial services. These limitations do not mean that higher levels of equity participation will not be possible in practice, but rather that the GATS commitment is limited to the amount specified. There are, however, certain sectors where Mexico has bound itself to allow 100 per cent ownership. These include certain professional services, all scheduled distribution services, and certain tourism and travel-related services.

NOTES

1 Statement by Mr. Herminio Blanco, Minister of International Trade of Mexico, 20 January 1994, GATT Document MTN.TNC/40/ST/17.

2 See Sam Laird (1995), Latin American Trade Liberalization, Minnesota Journal of Global Trade, vol. 4, issue 2. Measures not covered by Table 1 include reference prices, customs valuation procedures, supplementary and even discriminatory charges on imports, technical barriers and government procurement procedures.

3 GATT (1993), Trade Policy Review -- Mexico.

4 See J.F. Francois and Will Martin (1995), Multilateral Trade Rules and the Expected Cost of Protection, mimeo., -- an attempt to measure the impact of bindings on the expected cost of protection.

5 GATT (1993), Trade Policy Review -- Mexico.

6 See Richard Blackhurst, Alice Enders and Joseph Francois (1995), The Uruguay Round and Market Access: Opportunities and Challenges for Developing Countries, paper presented at the World Bank Conference on The Uruguay Round and the Developing Economies, 26-27 January, Washington D.C.

7 GATT (1993), Trade Policy Review -- Mexico, page 111.

8 GATT (1993), Trade Policy Review -- Mexico, Report by the Government of Mexico.

9 GATT (1993), Trade Policy Review -- Mexico, page 98.

10 GATT (1993), Trade Policy Review -- Mexico, Report by the Government of Mexico.

11 GATT (1993), Trade Policy Review -- Mexico, page 102.

12 GATT (1993), Trade Policy Review -- Mexico, page 91.

13   GATT (1993), Trade Policy Review -- Mexico.

14   GATT (1987), BISD 33S, pp. 80-81.

15   See P. Low and A. Subramanian (1995), TRIMs in the Uruguay Round: An Unfinished Business?, paper presented at the World Bank Conference on The Uruguay Round and the Developing Economies, 26-27 January, Washington D.C. for an analysis of such schemes.

16   The Mexican schedule also invariably includes in the context of commercial presence in financial services (a) restrictions on individual share-holding, usually stipulated not to exceed between 2.5 and 7.5 per cent, and (b) the requirement that effective control of the enterprise be with Mexican shareholders.

CHAPTER 6

SUMMARY AND CONCLUSIONS

This study has traced the evolution of Mexico from a closed, inward-looking economy in which the state played a prominent role, to a market-oriented open economy on the brink of establishing virtual free trade with several countries including the largest and one of the most competitive economies in the world. The study has focused primarily on trade policy, although many other aspects of Mexican economic policy have also been important in creating the necessary framework for fuller insertion into the world economy.

1. Mexico's reform programme

As noted in earlier chapters, Mexico began in the years following the 1982 debt crisis to dismantle the panoply of trade taxes and restrictions built up over the years that selectively restricted imports, allowing production for the domestic market behind high walls of protection and inhibiting exports. By the time the policy switch came, it is probable that Mexico was reaching the limits of import substitution policies in terms of their ability to generate continued growth. Import licenses were required for all imports until 1984. In that year, almost one-fifth of imports were relieved of licensing requirements. By the end of the next year, only one-third of imports required licenses, and now, ten years later, few licensing requirements remain. Tariffs were also reduced to a trade-weighted average of about 13 per cent by the time Mexico joined the GATT in 1986, and by 1987, the maximum tariff was 20 per cent. Minimum import prices for customs valuation purposes have been progressively removed. Mexico gradually eliminated its dual exchange rate regime during the 1980s, almost eradicating the spread between the two rates by the end of 1987, and finally abolishing the dual market in 1991. Exchange controls disappeared in 1987. This relatively open trade policy was consolidated and extended further following Mexico's decision to join NAFTA. Bearing in mind that

Mexico's North American trading partners accounted for around 85 per cent of Mexico's merchandise exports and some 72 per cent of its imports in 1993, the implications of the free trade commitment under NAFTA are far-reaching.

Trade liberalisation was by no means an isolated undertaking as far as Mexico's economic modernisation drive was concerned. The relaxation of historically rigid controls on FDI also played an essential role in injecting new capital into the economy, which helped to create jobs and contributed to growth. The 1993 Foreign Investment Law codified earlier measures to relax FDI restrictions and offered further investment opportunities and a continuing relaxation of bureaucratic prerequisites of foreign investment. Restrictions on FDI remain in certain sectors, but these restrictions are stated in a negative list, leaving all other sectors and activities automatically open to foreign investors, without any requirements for prior approval. This policy bore fruit, with new FDI increasing by some US$5 billion per annum from 1990 to 1994, representing on average an increase of over 10 per cent in the cumulative stock of investment in each of those years.

Mexico launched an active privatisation programme, virtually from 1982 onwards. While early privatisation efforts concentrated on numerous relatively small enterprises, it was not until the late 1980s that large enterprises in important sectors began to be transferred to the private sector. Among the sectors affected by privatisation after 1989 were banking, airlines, steel, telephone services, the railways, ports, electricity generation and distribution services, and some petrochemical industries. Deregulation has also represented a significant part of the government's effort to encourage the private sector and provide a friendly environment for conducting business.

Deregulation was made a priority from 1988, starting with the Salinas administration. Efforts to remove rent-generating restrictions and to eliminate bureaucratic red tape were mostly concentrated at the federal level. The sectors which were the centre of particular focus included road transport, airlines, port services, telecommunications, petrochemicals, and the financial sector. As noted above, most of these industries were also slated for privatisation. Alongside deregulation efforts, the government also developed trade facilitation arrangements aimed at dealing with administrative obstacles to exports as they arise. The so-called COMPEX mechanism consists of a series of committees constituted nationwide that hear specific complaints about government-generated barriers to exports. The committees must address such problems within a specified time-frame. The Zedillo administration intends to focus more on deregulation at the sub-federal (state and municipal) level, where it is perceived that many regulatory and bureaucratic barriers constitute obstacles to private sector activity.

The government has also adopted a number of pro-active policies in favour of exports and of small and medium-sized enterprises. In addition to the COMPEX programme and other efforts to minimise the costs of doing business that may be attributable to governmental procedures and regulations, export promotion efforts have focused largely on the dissemination of information and upon facilitating finance and credit to the trade sector. Programmes aimed at supporting small and medium enterprises include making certain kinds of training available and helping these enterprises to establish commercial links within the sectors in which they operate. None of these promotional efforts involve significant budgetary outlays and they are all broad-based, in the sense of not being targeted narrowly to benefit specific industries or firms. Indeed, they are the kinds of promotional activities found in virtually any country.

In 1993, the authorities established a law on competition and an independent Federal Competition Commission. This was a logical extension of the government's efforts to address those impediments to the proper functioning of markets for which it was responsible. If the government's own interventions were capable of generating anticompetitive effects, so too was the behaviour of private sector agents with any degree of monopolistic power. The competition authorities are empowered to address aspects of market behaviour and market structure that interfere with competition and make markets less contestable. The competition authorities have also been given a monitoring role with respect to government policy. The Commission is entitled to review and comment upon any government laws, regulations or actions from the point of view of their impact on competitive conditions in the market.

The government's trade and investment liberalisation efforts, together with its privatisation, deregulation, trade facilitation and competition policy initiatives can be thought of as a "market contestability package." A vital accompaniment of such a package is stabilisation policy. Market reforms are much less likely to be successful in the absence of macroeconomic stability. In effect, macroeconomic stability with growth was not attained until 1990, only to prove elusive again in late 1994 and early 1995. The sequence of policies and events underlying both the attainment of macroeconomic stability and its subsequent demise are documented in Chapter 2.

The crisis of late 1994 undoubtedly posed a threat to open trade policies, since the government might have been tempted to resort to protectionist measure in order to relieve the pressure on profits arising from the crisis. But this did not occur on a significant scale. Apart from the government's own philosophical disinclination to undo the hard-won trade liberalisation of recent years, two additional factors contributed to trade policy stability. One was the fact that the exchange rate was allowed to adjust, which engendered a substantial depreciation of the peso and quickly brought the current account into surplus. The other was that Mexico's trade liberalisation measures were tied in institutionally and politically through international commitments such as the WTO and several free trade agreements.

The importance of the latter factor would seem to be attested to by the fact that the government did make some trade policy adjustments outside the free trade agreements but within the WTO ambit -- tariffs were increased from prevailing rates of 20 per cent or less to 35 per cent on clothing, footwear and manufactured leather products on imports from non-preferential sources. These sectors were already protected to a certain degree through anti-dumping duties and a relatively restrictive use of marking and origin requirements. The policy flexibility inherent in maintaining tariffs at low applied rates, below WTO bound rates, is illustrated by the above measure. This situation may also illustrate the policy dilemma of pursuing unilateral liberalisation measures for which there is yet no "recognition" afforded at the multilateral level. In the absence of such "recognition", establishing a clear reduction trend of gap between bound and applied rates, by lowering bound rates, would provide more certainty at the multilateral level.

2. Controlling threats to open trade policies

Shortly after taking extensive trade-opening measures in 1985, in part as a prelude to GATT accession the following year, Mexico introduced anti-dumping and countervailing duty legislation. The use of these instruments by Mexico and several other countries (mainly developed) has not been free of controversy. Anti-dumping and countervailing duty actions are predicated on the assertion that trade is being unfairly conducted, either because firms located in the territory of a trading partner are selling at prices in export markets lower than those prevailing in the domestic market, or because governments are subsidising exports. On the anti-dumping front in particular, the notion that price discrimination between segmented markets represents a per se unfair trade practice has been widely criticised. There are many reasons why a producer may be able to sell products in different markets at different prices, and doing so does not automatically imply a predatory intent or a strategy for eliminating competition. Indeed, virtually no instance of predatory pricing behaviour has been documented in international markets, where competitive conditions frequently deny individual suppliers the requisite degree of market power to pursue such a strategy. Admittedly, the requirement that a government must establish that price discrimination (i.e. dumping) is causing or threatening material injury to a domestic injury may prevent anti-dumping duties from being imposed. On the other hand, it is well known that anti-dumping investigations are technically complex, and there will almost always be room for discretionary interpretations of one sort or another.

In these circumstances there is a risk anti-dumping may be used in a protectionist fashion, thus undermining the economic benefits of trade liberalisation by resort to spurious appeals for fairness. Used in excess, anti-dumping can indeed carry significant welfare costs, especially in countries where limited domestic competition exists within a sector, so that anti-dumping or countervailing actions that result in the suppression or elimination of foreign competition simply invite monopolistic behaviour on the part of domestic producers. On the other hand, from a political economy perspective, the existence of a safety valve, judiciously applied, may play a role in sustaining political support for a broad commitment to trade liberalisation. The balance is a delicate one.

From this perspective, it is arguable that a safeguard mechanism would be preferable to an unfair trade instrument. This is because safeguards do not impute unfair behaviour to trading partners, and the decision whether or not to grant relief to a domestic industry becomes an explicit matter of domestic economic policy. The costs and benefits of such action can then be assessed on their own merits, bearing in mind that protection for an industry carries costs for consumers or firms that use the protected product as an input. Although Mexico has established a safeguards mechanism under its Foreign Trade Law, it has virtually not been used. By contrast, almost 200 anti-dumping and countervailing duty cases were initiated between 1987 and 1995, and two-thirds of them have led to the imposition of duties. In the early 1990s, Mexico became a particularly intensive user of anti-dumping by international standards. The trade coverage of these instruments remains very modest, at less than one per cent of imports, but the mere threat of anti-dumping action can result in reduction or diversion of trade flows that are difficult to quantify. These measures can seriously inhibit trade and afford high margins of protection to domestic industry. For all countries contingency measures against imports should be used with a good deal of circumspection and greater emphasis should be accorded to safeguards as opposed to anti-dumping actions.

Complaints have arisen about imports being unnecessarily frustrated by the application of measures related to standards, marking, labelling and non-preferential rules of origin. These kinds of measures are essential to the proper conduct of trade, but they can also be designed or applied in a manner that restricts trade. This is contrary to the well-established principle that standards and related measures should not in and of themselves act as barriers to trade. Rather, they are administrative measures used to carry out underlying policies which may or may not be restrictive. Complaints have concerned standards that are considered more rigid than necessary, marking and labelling requirements that demand excessive information, and non-preferential origin rules to enforce anti-dumping and countervailing duties that impose a burden on producers and traders. No formal complaint has been submitted against Mexico within the Agreement on Technical Barriers to Trade, and it was beyond the scope of this study to investigate such claims in any detail, and so no judgement can be made as to whether they are justified. Nevertheless, the standards area is vulnerable to protectionist manipulation, and vigilance is required to ensure that measures are not designed or operated in a fashion that undermines the government's policy of maintaining open markets.

3.   Regionalism in trade relations

Mexico's embrace of regionalism has exerted a strong influence on trade policy and raises questions about coherence, the possible creation of trade distortions, the costs of administering overlapping regional arrangements, and the place of Mexico in the multilateral trading system. Before commenting on these matters, it is worthwhile considering the advantages of engaging in regional initiatives, and why Mexico may have chosen this course. Four principle considerations suggest themselves.

First, in a world where regional trading arrangements are multiplying, it is reasonable for countries to be concerned about the threat of exclusion. Establishing ties with one or more regional arrangements provides insurance against this. Moreover, as part of such arrangements, it may be easier to avoid or minimise the impact of protectionist measures taken by members of the grouping. Under NAFTA, for example, the special dispute settlement procedures of Chapter nineteen are intended to provide additional security in this respect. Second, membership to regional arrangements may help tie in domestic policy reforms, making them more difficult to reverse and making it easier for governments to avoid taking trade-restrictive action on the grounds that it would contravene an international agreement. This benefit could also be claimed for multilateral trade commitments, but regional agreements, such as NAFTA, often go further than multilateral commitments. This is the third reason for looking favourably upon regional agreements. Indeed, Mexico's membership of NAFTA implies eventual free trade, which is something not yet promised multilaterally, and NAFTA covers areas, such as investment, which is less developed at the multilateral level. Fourth, it is often easier to move more quickly to establish a regional agreement, and reap the benefits of liberalisation, since fewer countries are involved, and the negotiating parties will often have more similar views and aspirations than in a broader multilateral framework.

Certain potential costs and risks of regionalism have to be measured against these advantages. Regional arrangements can be inward-looking or outward-looking. If they are of the former variety, they may deny their members the benefits of liberalisation, leading to a kind of "lowest common denominator" outcome where the protectionist preferences of the members are traded off within the grouping. In the extreme, this can lead to a less liberal outcome compared to the pre-existing situation. Where the intent and design of a regional arrangement is of a more outward-looking persuasion, problems of trade diversion and the exclusion of third parties may also arise. Virtually all the commentaries that have been made on NAFTA appear to share the conclusion that it is a relatively open agreement, but some countries are concerned with one or two areas where the rules of origin may divert trade in favour of NAFTA members. NAFTA's consistency with WTO provisions is under examination. The recent increase of tariffs on clothing, footwear and manufactured leather products for non-preferential imports may also reinforce the argument of potential trade diversion effects for non participating parties to regional trading arrangements.

A potential difficulty facing countries like Mexico, which are involved in a range of overlapping agreements, is that these agreements could become mutually inconsistent, and create additional obstacles for producers and traders that operate internationally in different locations. The increasing globalisation of economic activity could make a multiplicity of arrangements a hazard in such circumstances. Difficulties and extra costs can also multiply for governments as they try to administer different agreements. While it may be impossible to avoid these problems altogether, they can certainly be kept to a minimum by ensuring that discrete agreements do not differ greatly in terms of the specifics of their provisions. If different regional agreements share the common objective of opening markets and creating new economic opportunities, it should not prove too difficult to attain a high degree of uniformity. This certainly seems to be the pattern as far as Mexico's free trade agreements with North, Central and South America are concerned.

Finally, if regionalism is to be broadly compatible with multilateralism, so that discriminatory and exclusive trading arrangements do not come to dominate international trade, it is important that regional groupings be open in the sense of not excluding potential new members. In Mexico's case, even if no other countries besides Chile join NAFTA in the near future, the fact that Mexico has entered into NAFTA-like agreements with several of its trading partners may arguably achieve something similar to NAFTA enlargement, as least as far as Mexico's trade relations are concerned. Moreover, Mexico's willingness to engage in the exploration of a broader free trade initiative throughout the Western Hemisphere, to participate in the Asia Pacific Economic Co-operation (APEC), and to consider similar arrangements with Western Europe, clearly points to a determination to avoid geographically-constrained market opening.

At the same time, the WTO forum provides an essential backdrop against which regional initiatives should be conducted, and governments should be careful not to ignore their multilateral obligations, or to permit the multilateral forum to suffer from neglect. A multilateral forum is essential for all countries, not only so that they can conduct their trade relations in an orderly fashion with countries that are not members of their regional groupings, but also because situations are bound to arise where the multilateral mediation of differences arising in a regional context may prove invaluable. Mexico's participation in the Uruguay Round and acceptance of commitments under the WTO suggests that the government is well aware of the importance of maintaining a multilateral component in its international economic relations.

LIST OF TABLES

Table 1. Liberalisation of trade restrictions
(per cent)

	1983	1984	1985	1986	1987	1988	1989	1990	1991	1992	1993	1994
Import license coverage[1]	100	83	35.1	27.8	26.8	21.2	14.0	13.7	9.1	10.7	21.5	12.97
Reference prices[2]	13.4	13.4	25.4	18.6	13.4	0	0	0	0	0	0	0
Tariffs:												
Simple average	27	23.3	25.4	22.6	10.0	9.7	13.1	13.1	13.1	13.1	13.0	12.4
Trade weighted average	16.4	8.5	13.3	13.1	5.6	6.2	10.1	10.5	11.2	11.5	11.6	11.0
Tariff positions	16	10	10	11	5	5	5	5	5	6	6	8
Maximum tariff	100	100	100	100	20	20	20	20	20	25	25	25

1. Percentage of imports covered.
2. Percentage of 1986 production covered.
Source: SECOFI and Banco de Mexico

Table 2. Merchandise exports

	1987	1990	1991	1992	1993	1994	1995 (Jan.-June)	Growth rates 1987-94
(US$ millions)								
Total	**27 600**	**40 711**	**42 949**	**46 196**	**51 886**	**60 834**	**38 312**	**11.95**
Petroleum	8 630	10 104	8 166	8 307	7 418	7 393	4 281	-2.19
Non-petroleum	18 970	30 607	34 782	37 889	44 468	53 440	34 030	15.95
Agriculture	1 543	2 162	2 373	2 112	2 504	2 678	2 750	8.19
Mining	576	617	547	356	278	357	274	-6.61
Manufacturing	16 851	27 828	31 863	35 421	41 685	50 423	31 007	16.95
Maquiladora	7 105	13 873	15 828	18 680	21 853	26 269	14 516	20.54
Non-maquiladora	9 746	13 956	16 035	16 740	19 832	24 136	16 491	13.83
(per cent)								
Total	**100**	**100**	**100**	**100**	**100**	**100**	**100**	
Petroleum	31.27	24.82	19.01	17.98	14.30	12.15	11.17	
Non-petroleum	68.73	75.18	80.98	82.02	85.70	87.85	88.82	
Agriculture	5.59	5.31	5.53	4.57	4.83	4.40	7.18	
Mining	2.09	1.52	1.27	0.77	0.54	0.59	0.72	
Manufacturing	61.05	68.35	74.19	76.68	80.34	82.89	80.93	
Maquiladora	25.74	34.08	36.85	40.44	42.12	43.18	37.89	
Non-maquiladora	35.31	34.28	37.33	36.24	38.22	39.68	43.04	

Note: Due to the rounding-off of figures, totals might not equal the sum of their components.
Source: Banco de Mexico

Table 3. Structure of non-maquiladora manufactured exports

(per cent)

	1981	1985	1986	1987	1988	1989	1990	1991	1992	1993
All manufacturing	100	100	100	100	100	100	100	100	100	100
Food, drink and tobacco	19.82	11.11	8.70	12.40	11.06	9.74	7.41	6.15	6.45	6.99
Textiles and apparel	4.38	2.72	2.83	4.53	4.12	3.89	3.38	3.12	3.94	4.39
Leather and hides	0.91	0.36	0.29	0.81	0.94	0.90	0.90	0.75	1.15	1.81
Wood and wooden products	1.73	1.36	0.97	1.27	1.47	1.52	1.14	0.96	1.34	1.88
Paper and printing	2.37	1.47	1.27	2.10	2.62	2.07	1.37	1.18	1.24	0.27
Petroleum derivatives	17.83	20.09	5.84	5.97	4.99	3.26	6.04	3.25	3.57	3.18
Petrochemicals	3.87	1.59	0.80	1.14	1.68	1.23	1.97	1.31	1.51	0.91
Chemicals	13.34	10.06	7.58	10.32	11.29	11.81	11.36	10.00	12.01	8.55
Plastics and rubber	0.66	0.75	0.73	1.06	1.26	1.37	0.86	0.88	0.90	0.56
Non-metallic minerals	3.64	4.69	3.43	4.22	4.25	4.35	3.55	3.19	3.86	4.12
Steel	1.87	3.66	4.08	5.95	6.13	6.66	6.59	5.07	4.97	1.30
Metallurgy	2.05	6.00	4.33	5.95	6.61	7.94	6.51	3.80	4.83	3.49
Transportation	13.84	24.04	18.74	31.67	28.75	29.28	31.52	44.45	34.98	38.58
Machinery and equipment	14.05	12.11	40.41	12.60	14.84	15.98	17.41	15.89	19.26	23.95

Source: Banco Nacional de Comercio Exterior

Table 4. Structure of maquiladora exports

(per cent)

	1992	1993	1994	1995 (Jan.-May)
All manufacturing	**100**	**100**	**100**	**100**
Food, drink and tobacco	1.26	1.04	0.93	0.92
Textiles, apparel and leather	7.65	8.19	8.02	8.70
Wood and wooden products	1.42	1.40	1.22	1.05
Paper and printing	2.35	2.16	1.26	1.14
Petroleum derivatives	0.00	0.00	0.00	0.00
Petrochemicals	0.00	0.00	0.00	0.00
Chemicals	1.07	1.04	1.04	1.05
Plastics and rubber	3.41	3.62	2.93	2.64
Non-metallic minerals	1.31	1.47	1.38	1.30
Steel	1.48	1.52	1.18	1.08
Metallurgy	0.46	0.36	0.29	0.24
Machinery and equipment	76.87	76.55	78.62	78.61
Other manufactures	2.10	2.66	3.13	3.29

Note: Due to the rounding-off of figures, totals might not equal the sum of their components.
Source: Banco de Mexico

Table 5. Merchandise imports

	1987	1990	1991	1992	1993	1994	1995 (Jan.-June)	Growth rates 1987-94
(US$ millions)								
Total imports	**18 812.4**	**41 593.4**	**49 878.3**	**62 129.4**	**65 366.5**	**79 374.0**	**35 223.0**	**22.83**
Consumer goods	767.6	5 098.6	5 639.5	7 744.1	7 842.4	9 511.0	2 666.0	43.27
Intermediary goods	15 414.2	29 705.2	35 768.2	42 829.6	46 468.3	56 542.0	28 123.0	20.40
Maquiladora	5 507.0	10 321.4	11 694.3	13 936.7	16 443.0	20 494.0	12 315.0	20.65
Other	9 907.2	19 383.8	24 073.9	28 892.8	30 025.3	36 049.0	15 804.0	20.26
Capital goods	2 630.6	6 789.6	8 470.6	11 555.7	11 055.9	13 322.0	4 435.0	26.08
(per cent)								
Total imports	**100**	**100**	**100**	**100**	**100**	**100**	**100**	
Consumer goods	4.08	12.26	11.31	12.46	12.00	11.98	7.57	193.67
Intermediary goods	81.94	71.42	71.71	68.94	71.09	71.23	79.84	-13.06
Maquiladora	29.27	24.81	23.45	22.43	25.16	25.82	34.96	-11.80
Other	52.66	46.60	48.27	46.50	45.93	45.42	44.87	-13.76
Capital goods	13.98	16.32	16.98	18.60	16.91	16.78	12.59	20.03

Source: Banco de Mexico

118

Table 6A. Composition of exports
(US$ millions)

EXPORTS	1992 Maqui-ladora	1992 non maqui-ladora	Total
TOTAL	**18 680**	**27 516**	**46 196**
Petroleum	0	8 307	8 307
Crude	0	7 420	7 420
Others	0	887	887
Non-petroleum	18 680	19 209	37 889
Agriculture	0	2 112	2 112
Mining	0	356	356
Manufacturing	18 680	16 740	35 420
Food, drink and tobacco	234	1 131	1 365
Textiles and apparel	1 428	889	2 317
Leather and hides	265	234	499
Paper and printing	438	217	655
Chemicals	195	2 099	2 294
Plastics and rubber	637	158	795
Non-metallic minerals	245	674	919
Steel	277	868	1 145
Metallurgy	86	843	929
Machinery and equipment	14 345	9 367	23 712
Agriculture	29	19	48
Ferrous	0	15	15
Transportation	1 265	6 091	7 356
Non-electrical equipment	1 932	1 751	3 683
Scientific equipment	510	37	547
Electrical equipment	10 476	1 253	11 729
Photographic equipment	132	200	332
Other industries	527	261	788

.../..

Table 6A. (cont'd.) Composition of exports
(US$ millions)

| EXPORTS | 1994 | | |
	Maqui-ladora	Non maqui-ladora	Total
TOTAL	**26 269**	**34 613**	**60 882**
Petroleum	0	7 445	7 445
Crude	0	6 624	6 624
Others	0	821	821
Non-petroleum	26 269	27 168	53 437
Agriculture	0	2 678	2 678
Mining	0	357	357
Manufacturing	26 269	24 133	50 402
Food, drink and tobacco	243	1 653	1 896
Textiles and apparel	2 106	1 150	3 256
Leather and hides	319	267	586
Paper and printing	332	229	561
Chemicals	274	2 482	2 756
Plastics and rubber	771	294	1 065
Non-metallic minerals	361	854	1 215
Steel	311	1 224	1 535
Metallurgy	76	1 010	1 086
Machinery and equipment	20 651	14 674	35 325
Agriculture	77	29	106
Ferrous	0	19	19
Transportation	2 043	8 824	10 867
Non-electrical equipment	2 952	3 055	6 007
Scientific equipment	614	38	652
Electrical equipment	14 850	2 456	17 276
Photographic equipment	114	282	396
Other industries	826	297	1 123

Note: Due to the rounding-off of figures, totals might not equal the sum of their components.

Source: Annual Report 1994, Banco de Mexico

Table 6B. Composition of imports
(US$ millions)

IMPORTS	1992 Maqui-ladora	1992 non maqui-ladora	Total
TOTAL	**13 937**	**48 192**	**62 129**
Consumer goods	0	7 744	7 744
Intermediary goods	13 937	28 893	42 830
Agriculture	31	2 466	2 497
Mining	15	505	520
Manufacturing	13 891	25 922	39 813
Food, drink and tobacco	57	1 064	1 121
Textiles and apparel	1 056	815	1 871
Leather and hides	139	400	539
Paper and printing	609	1 136	1 745
Derived petroleum	14	557	571
Petrochemicals	7	506	513
Chemicals	433	3 647	4 080
Plastics and rubber	1 762	1 231	2 993
Non-metallic minerals	181	433	614
Steel	993	2 268	3 261
Metallurgy	241	807	1 048
Machinery and equipment	7 971	12 800	20 771
Agriculture	3	13	16
Ferrous	1	35	36
Transport	486	723	8 009
Non electrical equipment	1 319	2 724	4 043
Scientific equipment	130	83	213
Electrical equipment	5 977	2 255	8 232
Photographic equipment	57	167	224
Other industries	431	258	689
Capital goods	0	11 556	11 556

.../..

Table 6B. (Cont'd.) Composition of imports
(US$ millions)

IMPORTS	1994 Maqui-ladora	1994 Non maqui-ladora	Total
TOTAL	**20 466**	**58 880**	**79 346**
Consumer goods	0	9 510	9 510
Intermediary goods	20 466	36 048	56 514
Agriculture	40	2 729	2 769
Mining	17	421	438
Manufacturing	20 409	32 898	53 307
Food, drink and tobacco	36	1 102	1 138
Textiles and apparel	1 817	1 118	2 936
Leather and hides	172	498	671
Paper and printing	748	1 647	2 395
Derived petroleum	12	636	647
Petrochemicals	14	745	759
Chemicals	562	4 652	5 214
Plastics and rubber	2 009	1 822	3 832
Non-metallic minerals	286	599	885
Steel	1 277	2 443	3 720
Metallurgy	351	843	1 195
Machinery and equipment	12 046	16 278	28 324
Agriculture	3	22	25
Ferrous	0	64	64
Transport	597	8 929	9 525
Non electrical equipment	1 769	3 775	5 545
Scientific equipment	268	131	400
Electrical equipment	9 294	3 160	12 454
Photographic equipment	115	196	311
Other industries	1 077	516	1 592
Capital goods	0	13 322	13 322

Note: Due to the rounding-off of figures, totals might not equal the sum of their components.

Source: Annual Report 1994, Banco de Mexico

Table 7. Structure of maquiladora imports

(per cent)

	1992	1993	1994	1995 (Jan.-May)
All Manufacturing	**100**	**100**	**100**	**100**
Food, drink and tobacco	0.42	0.27	0.19	0.11
Textiles, apparel and leather	7.76	8.80	9.27	9.40
Wood and wooden products	1.02	0.99	0.88	0.75
Paper and printing	4.47	3.79	3.82	3.63
Petroleum derivatives	0.10	0.09	0.06	0.06
Petrochemicals	0.05	0.09	0.08	0.07
Chemicals	3.18	2.85	2.87	3.00
Plastics and rubber	12.95	11.86	10.25	10.07
Non-metallic minerals	1.33	1.35	1.46	1.48
Steel	7.30	6.99	6.51	6.01
Metallurgy	1.77	1.59	1.79	1.84
Machinery and equipment	58.60	60.20	61.57	62.50
Other manufactures	1.06	1.02	1.27	1.07

Note: Due to the rounding-off of figures, totals might not equal the sum of their components.
Source: Banco de Mexico

123

Table 8. Non-maquiladora trade balance

(US$ millions)

	1985	1988	1989	1990	1991	1992	1993
Total	**8 406**	**1 754**	**-645**	**-2 996**	**-11 064**	**-20 608**	**-18 535**
Agriculture and forestry	-165	4	-285	-101	214	-665	-363
Ranching	-135	-131	-3	157	-9	-62	195
Hunting and fishing	4	25	40	43	75	46	39
Mining	13 606	6 220	7 509	9 151	7 414	7 245	6 320
Petroleum and natural gas	13 305	5 874	7 252	8 895	7 234	7 236	6 342
Manufacturing	-4 812	-4 366	-7 789	-12 242	-18 722	-27 061	-24 726
Food, beverages and tobacco	236	137	-746	-1 584	-1 368	-2 151	-1 767
Textiles and apparel	44	97	-194	-424	-585	-982	-2 165
Hides and leather	9	77	4	8	-45	-96	14
Wood products	34	101	87	-6	-96	-178	3
Paper and printing	-335	-473	-666	-858	-1 036	-1 363	-1 704
Petroleum derivatives	702	114	-389	-165	-620	-768	-649
Petrochemicals	-584	-456	-392	-28	-215	-243	-386
Chemicals	-696	-485	-920	-1 098	-1 369	-1 881	-2 511
Plastics and rubber	-207	-312	-449	-658	-927	-1 233	-1 398
Non-metallic minerals	209	366	338	213	228	138	306
Steel	-507	-330	-445	-655	-1 187	-1 601	-1 914
Metallurgy	23	409	569	518	211	70	56
Transportation vehicles and parts	85	989	1 342	12	1 064	-3 298	-1 483
Other machinery and equipment	-3 821	-4 600	-5 929	-7 519	-9 777	-13 476	-21 101

Note: Due to the rounding-off of figures, totals might not equal the sum of their components.
Source: Banco Nacional de Comercio Exterior

Table 9. Maquiladora trade balance
(US$ millions)

	1992	1993	1994	1995 (Jan.-May)
All manufacturing	**5 058.2**	**5 974.7**	**6 656.5**	**2 111.1**
Food, drink and tobacco	177.3	183.6	206.8	97.2
Textiles, apparel and leather	372.1	391.4	288	115.7
Wood and wooden products	126.3	147.1	147.1	50.9
Paper and printing	-170.9	-129.2	-416	-216.4
Petroleum derivatives	-13.7	-14.9	-11.6	-5.8
Petrochemicals	-6.9	-13.8	-14.9	-7.2
Chemicals	-233.4	-225	-287.9	-166.0
Plastics and rubber	-1 125.5	-1 090.4	-1 238.7	-661.5
Non-metallic minerals	64.6	107.3	75.3	9.2
Steel	-715.6	-778.1	-966.6	-452.6
Metallurgy	-154.9	-174.2	-275.8	-149.4
Machinery and equipment	6 373.3	7 169.8	8 577.3	3 213.7
Other manufactures	-125.5	419.3	572.5	283.4

Source: Banco de Mexico

Table 10. Services trade
(US$ millions)

	1985	1990	1991	1992	1993	1994 [1]
Exports	**8 640.7**	**14 677**	**15 154**	**15 107**	**14 759**	**11 756**
Non-factor services	4 677.6	7 961.6	8 790.1	9 191.8	9 352.6	7 124.9
Transportation	577.2	892.9	900.7	980.7	937.9	744.2
Overseas	1 719.7	3 400.9	4 339.3	4 471.1	4 564.1	3 509.4
Border tourism	1 180.6	2 066.1	1 619.8	1 613.7	1 602.9	1 115.2
Other	1 200.1	1 601.8	1 930.3	2 126.2	2 247.7	1 755.9
Factor services	2 135.7	3 236.7	3 599.6	2 876	2 702.9	2 399.8
Interest	1 821.7	2 667	2 905.9	2 159.6	1 960.9	1 847.2
Other	314	569.7	693.7	716.4	742	552.7
Transfers	1 827.4	3 479	2 764.3	3 039.6	2 703.5	2 231.9
Imports	**16 325**	**20 908**	**22 767**	**23 978**	**24 671**	**17 105**
Non-factor services	5 262.9	9 942.2	10 541	11 488	11 028	8 388.6
Insurance	550.3	1 530.8	1 758.0	2 084.0	2 180.7	1 923.0
Transportation	842.4	1 132.5	1 270.6	1 350.1	1 360.1	1 034.4
Overseas	664.3	1 936.5	2 149.8	2 541.7	2 416.6	1 827
Border tourism	1 594.4	3 582.2	3 663.1	3 565.8	3 145.2	2 074.3
Other	1 611.5	1 760.1	1 699.5	1 946.5	1 925.7	1 529.9
Factor services	11 034	1 0952	12 207	12 470	13 626	8 705.4
Repatriated	386.3	661.1	1 084	1 293	1 412	1 205.7
Reinvested	231.8	653.6	1 408	1 020	1 135	1 014.4
Interest	10 155	9 194.6	9 215.2	9 610.6	10 507	9 036.3
Commission	38.1	63.4	81.4	75.7	76.7	77.6
Other	222.2	380.1	419.1	471.5	495.2	371.1
Transfers	28.3	14	18.9	19.2	16.5	11.6
Balance	**-7 684.3**	**-6 231**	**-7 613**	**-8 871**	**-9 912**	**-5 349**
Non-factor services	-585.3	-1 980.6	-1 750.9	-2 296.2	-1 675.4	-1 263.7
Insurance	-550.3	1 530.8	1 758.0	2 084.0	2 180.7	1 923.0
Transportation	-265.2	-239.6	-369.9	-369.4	-422.2	-290.2
Overseas	1 055.4	1 464.4	2 189.5	1 929.4	2 147.5	1 682.4
Border tourism	-413.8	-1 516.1	-2 043.3	-1 952.1	-1 542.3	-959.1
Other	-411.4	-158.3	230.8	179.7	322	226
Factor services	-8 898.3	-7 715.3	-8 607.4	-9 594.0	-10 923.1	-6 305.6
Repatriated	-386.3	-661.1	-1 084.0	-1 293.0	-1 412.0	-1 205.7
Reinvested	-2 31.8	-653.6	-1 408.0	-1 020.0	-1 135.0	-1 014.4
Interest	-8 327.6	-6 527.6	-6 309.3	-7 451.0	-8 546.1	-7 189.1
Commission	-38.1	-63.4	-81.4	-75.7	-76.7	-77.6
Other	91.8	189.6	274.6	244.9	246.8	181.6
Transfers	1 799.1	3 465	2 745.4	3 020.4	2 687	2 220.3

1.   January - October.
Source: Banco de Mexico

Table 11. Bilateral merchandise exports
(US$ millions)

	1985	1990	1991	1992[1]	1993[1]
Total	**21 866.0**	**26 838.0**	**27 120.0**	**46 195.0**	**51 886.0**
North America	13 768.0	19 227.0	19 469.0	38 419.0	44 609.0
Canada	393.4	230.6	1 125.2	999.7	1 541.5
United States	13 374.0	18 997.0	18 344.0	37 419.0	43 067.0
Central American Common Market	269.2	345.4	411.3	477.6	473.8
Costa Rica	21.0	64.4	79.8	106.9	99.3
El Salvador	88.4	106.4	116.1	120.5	112.1
Guatemala	101.2	108.2	141.9	153.2	203.8
Honduras	28.3	53.4	55.3	78.5	37.9
Nicaragua	30.3	13.0	18.3	18.3	20.7
Latin American Free Trade Association, of which:	597.4	883.1	987.0	1 361.3	1 585.5
Argentina	36.7	115.0	185.5	179.7	278.1
Brazil	297.8	169.0	187.4	408.1	290.8
Chile	16.4	91.1	126.8	152.4	194.0
Andean Group	221.8	373.8	432.5	551.7	630.7
Bolivia	0.2	3.9	12.7	8.5	17.0
Colombia	121.2	110.3	155.7	218.7	235.9
Ecuador	48.3	57.1	59.9	62.5	56.4
Peru	13.0	65.8	77.6	62.7	94.0
Venezuela	39.1	136.7	126.6	199.3	227.4
Caribbean Common Market	53.6	105.3	112.2	157.7	118.2
Other American Countries, of which:	361.3	532.9	621.4	743.7	881.0
Cuba	69.7	104.8	105.7	116.9	188.2
Panama	119.3	71.5	99.2	108.7	145.1
Dominican Republic	132.0	107.6	149.6	178.4	203.0
European Union	4 025.1	3 398.7	3 219.8	3 299.1	2 600.1
European Free Trade Association	75.0	250.6	193.8	236.7	210.3
Eastern European Countries	56.7	36.3	33.7	17.3	18.3
Other Countries	2 659.9	2 058.4	1 999.0	1 482.2	1 389.6
Japan	1 709.1	1 449.1	1 240.9	793.5	700.4

1. These years include maquiladora trade. Previous years do not include maquiladora trade.
Note: Due to the rounding-off of figures, totals might not equal the sum of their components.
Source: Banco Nacional de Comercio Exterior

Table 12. Bilateral merchandise imports
(US$ millions)

	1985	1990	1991	1992[1]	1993[1]
Total	**13 460.0**	**31 271.0**	**38 184.0**	**62 129.0**	**65 366.0**
North America	9 142.5	20 912.0	25 667.0	45 267.0	47 630.0
Canada	235.4	459.4	764.3	1 051.7	1 163.3
United States	8 907.1	20 452.0	24 903.0	44 216.0	46 466.0
Central American Common Market	30.5	102.2	146.4	125.9	114.1
Costa Rica	8.2	38.4	20.6	14.5	21.8
El Salvador	0.4	3.4	19.3	11.8	14.1
Guatemala	16.0	40.6	86.9	77.2	61.3
Honduras	5.8	2.4	5.5	4.8	5.5
Nicaragua	0.1	17.4	14.0	17.6	11.4
Latin American Free Trade Association of which:	564.8	1 222.7	1 529.6	2 032.9	2 153.7
Argentina	268.8	401.6	364.8	240.8	250.1
Brazil	203.6	422.9	753.5	1 108.7	1 192.5
Chile	52.0	61.2	49.8	95.5	129.9
Andean Group	32.3	304.7	325.8	536.9	533.6
Bolivia	1.0	4.9	10.2	17.1	16.2
Colombia	5.2	34.5	49.7	72.3	83.4
Ecuador	2.0	16.4	23.3	49.8	37.1
Peru	10.6	75.9	102.3	190.3	169.9
Venezuela	13.5	172.4	140.3	207.3	226.9
Caribbean Common Market	3.2	6.4	22.1	46.4	50.0
Other American Countries, of which:	78.4	235.3	222.8	211.1	228.3
Cuba	2.3	83.7	44.4	7.6	7.1
Panama	19.8	87.8	92.9	57.7	60.6
Dominican Republic	0.0	1.8	2.3	3.9	3.3
European Union	1 525.1	4 686.2	5 703.1	7 154.5	7 287.7
European Free Trade Association	336.3	787.1	891.7	1 025.7	944.2
Eastern European Countries	43.7	135.9	160.1	152.5	196.4
Other Countries	1 736.0	3 183.8	3 820.9	6 112.7	6 762.0
Japan	723.3	1 432.4	2 030.7	3 040.6	3 368.9

1.   These years include maquiladora trade. Previous years do not include maquiladora trade.

Note: Due to the rounding-off of figures, totals might not equal the sum of their components.

Source: Banco Nacional de Comercio Exterior

Table 13. Bilateral merchandise trade balance
(US$ millions)

	1985	1990	1991	1992[1]	1993[1]
Total	**8 406.0**	**-4 433.5**	**-11 063.8**	**-15 933.8**	**-13 480.6**
North America	4 625.8	-1 684.4	-6 197.3	-6 848.7	-3 021.0
Canada	158.0	-228.8	360.9	-52.0	378.2
United States	4 467.8	-1 455.6	-6 558.2	-6 796.7	-3 399.2
Central American Common Market	238.7	243.1	265.0	351.7	359.7
Costa Rica	12.7	26	59.2	92.4	77.5
El Salvador	88	103.0	96.8	108.7	98.1
Guatemala	85.2	67.6	55.0	76.0	142.5
Honduras	22.5	51.0	49.8	73.7	32.3
Nicaragua	30.2	-4.4	4.2	0.7	9.3
Latin American Free Trade Association of which:	32.6	-339.6	-542.6	-671.6	-568.2
Argentina	-232.1	-286.6	-179.3	-61.1	28.1
Brazil	94.2	-253.9	-566.1	-700.6	-901.7
Chile	-35.7	29.9	77.0	56.9	64.1
Andean Group	188.4	69.7	106.7	14.8	97.2
Bolivia	-0.9	-1.0	2.5	-8.6	0.9
Colombia	115.9	75.8	106.0	146.4	152.5
Ecuador	46.3	40.7	36.6	12.7	19.3
Peru	2.4	-10.2	-24.7	-127.6	-76.0
Venezuela	25.6	-35.7	-13.7	-8.0	0.5
Caribbean Common Market	50.4	98.9	90.2	111.3	68.2
Other American Countries, of which:	282.9	297.6	398.7	532.6	652.7
Cuba	67.4	21.1	61.2	109.3	181.2
Panama	99.6	-16.2	6.3	51.0	84.4
Dominican Republic	131.9	105.8	147.4	174.5	199.7
European Union	2 500.1	-1 287.5	-2 411.3	-3 855.4	-4 687.6
European Free Trade Association	-261.3	-536.5	-697.9	-789.0	-734.0
Eastern European Countries	13.0	-99.6	-126.5	-135.2	-178.0
Other Countries	923.9	-1 125.4	-1 821.9	-4 629.8	-5 372.4
Japan	985.8	16.6	-789.8	-2 247.1	-2 668.5

1.   These years include maquiladora trade. Previous years do not include maquiladora trade.
Note: Due to the rounding-off of figures, totals might not equal the sum of their components.
Source: Banco Nacional de Comercio Exterior

Table 14. Cumulative foreign direct investment by sector

	New investment	Cumulative investment	By sector: Industry	Services	Commerce	Mining	Agriculture
(US$ millions)							
1982	627	10 786	8 347	1 272	926	237	5
1983	684	11 470	8 944	1 285	984	252	5
1984	1 430	12 900	10 213	1 407	1 016	258	6
1985	1 729	14 629	11 379	1 842	1 125	276	6
1986	2 424	17 053	13 298	2 165	1 277	307	6
1987	3 877	20 930	15 699	3 599	1 255	356	22
1988	3 157	24 087	16 719	5 477	1 502	381	10
1989	2 500	26 587	17 701	6 579	1 889	390	29
1990	3 722	30 310	18 894	8 782	2 060	484	90
1991	3 650	33 875	19 857	10 920	2 447	515	135
1992	3 599	37 473	20 958	15 620	3 198	524	174
1993	4 901	42 374	23 279	14 351	3 958	579	209
1994	8 026	50 401	26 483	18 517	4 594	591	217
1995[1]	3 722	54 123	27 382	20 853	5 066	603	218

	New investment	Cumulative investment	By Sector: Industry	Services	Commerce	Mining	Agriculture
(per cent)							
1982	5.81	100	77.39	11.79	8.59	2.20	0.05
1983	5.96	100	77.98	11.20	8.58	2.20	0.04
1984	11.09	100	79.17	10.91	7.88	2.00	0.05
1985	11.82	100	77.78	12.59	7.69	1.89	0.04
1986	14.21	100	77.98	12.70	7.49	1.80	0.04
1987	18.52	100	75.01	17.20	6.00	1.70	0.11
1988	13.11	100	69.41	22.74	6.24	1.58	0.04
1989	9.40	100	66.58	24.75	7.10	1.47	0.11
1990	12.28	100	62.34	28.97	6.80	1.60	0.30
1991	10.71	100	58.62	32.24	7.22	1.52	0.40
1992	9.60	100	55.93	41.68	8.53	1.40	0.46
1993	11.57	100	54.94	33.87	9.34	1.37	0.49
1994	15.92	100	52.54	36.74	9.11	1.17	0.43
1995[1]	6.88	100	50.59	38.53	9.36	1.11	0.40

1.   Figures for January and February.

Source: SECOFI

130

Table 15. Cumulative foreign direct investment by country of origin

(US$ millions)	TOTAL	U.S.A.	Canada	U.K.	Germany	Switzerland	Japan	France	Others
1983	**11 470**	7 601	162	351	973	588	780	229	786
1984	**12 900**	8 513	195	396	1 125	648	816	237	970
1985	**14 629**	9 840	230	452	1 181	789	895	248	994
1986	**17 053**	11 047	270	556	1 399	823	1 038	565	1 355
1987	**20 930**	13 716	290	987	1 446	918	1 170	596	1 807
1988	**24 087**	14 958	324	1 754	1 583	1 005	1 319	749	2 395
1989	**26 587**	16 772	361	1 799	1 668	1 199	1 335	765	2 688
1990	**30 310**	19 080	417	1 914	1 956	1 347	1 456	946	3 194
1991	**33 875**	21 466	791	1 988	2 041	1 415	1 529	1 447	3 198
1992	**37 473**	23 118	580	2 414	2 126	1 730	1 616	1 516	4 373
1993	**42 375**	26 622	654	2 603	2 237	1 832	1 690	1 593	5 143
1994	**50 401**	30 626	817	3 703	2 612	1 885	2 390	1 656	6 713
1995[1]	**54 123**	31 971	1 338	3 723	2 690	1 811	2 403	1 681	8 435

(per cent)	TOTAL	U.S.A.	Canada	U.K.	Germany	Switzerland	Japan	France	Others
1983	**100**	66.27	1.41	3.06	8.48	5.13	6.80	2.00	6.85
1984	**100**	65.99	1.51	3.07	8.72	5.02	6.33	1.84	7.52
1985	**100**	67.26	1.57	3.09	8.07	5.39	6.12	1.70	6.79
1986	**100**	64.78	1.58	3.26	8.20	4.83	6.09	3.31	7.95
1987	**100**	65.53	1.39	4.72	6.91	4.39	5.59	2.85	8.63
1988	**100**	62.10	1.35	7.28	6.57	4.17	5.48	3.11	9.94
1989	**100**	63.08	1.36	6.77	6.27	4.51	5.02	2.88	10.11
1990	**100**	62.95	1.38	6.31	6.45	4.44	4.80	3.12	10.54
1991	**100**	63.37	2.34	5.87	6.03	4.18	4.51	4.27	9.44
1992	**100**	61.69	1.55	6.44	5.67	4.62	4.31	4.05	11.67
1993	**100**	62.82	1.54	6.14	5.28	4.32	3.99	3.76	12.14
1994	**100**	60.76	1.62	7.26	5.18	3.74	4.74	3.28	13.32
1995[1]	**100**	59.07	2.47	6.88	4.97	3.48	4.44	3.11	15.59

1.   Figures for January and February.
Source: SECOFI

131

Table 16. Mexico's MFN import regime as of 31 December 1993

(Import figures in billions of US$)

Tariff	All imports			Subject to import licenses			Not subject to import licenses		
	Number of tariff lines	%	Value of imports	%	Number of tariff lines	%	Value of imports	%	Number of tariff lines	%	Value of imports	%
0	411	3.5	6 456	14.7	12	6.3	1 713	18.1	399	3.4	4 742	13.80
5	85	0.7	283	0.6	3	1.6	14	0.2	82	0.7	268	0.80
10	5 690	48.2	19 199	43.7	109	56.7	6 985	73.8	5 581	48.0	12 213	35.48
15	3 232	27.4	9 101	20.7	2	1.0	37	0.4	3 230	27.8	9 074	26.30
20	2 395	20.3	8 807	20.0	66	34.4	716	7.6	2 329	20.0	8 091	23.50
25	3	0.0	74	0.2	0	0.0	0	0.0	3	0.0	74	0.20
Total	**11 816**	**100.0**	**43 932**	**100.0**	**192**	**100.0**	**9 467**	**100.0**	**11 624**	**100.0**	**34 464**	**100.0**
% of all imports	100		100		1.6		21.6		98.4		78.4	
Tariff Summary Data												
Simple average	13.0				12.8				13.0			
Dispersion	4.7				5.6				4.6			
Weighted average	11.6				9.0				12.3			
Weighted dispersion	6.2				5.0				6.3			

Note: 17 tariff lines of prohibited products and 8 tariff lines for sugar are not included.
Source: SECOFI

Table 17. Mexico's MFN import regime as of 31 December 1994
(Import figures in millions of US$)

Tariff	All imports				Subject to import licenses				Not subject to import licenses			
	Number of tariff lines	%	Value of imports	%	Number of tariff lines	%	Value of imports	%	Number of tariff lines	%	Value of imports	%
Non-agricultural products												
0	1 068	6.3	10 496	23.5	18	15.3	1 091	21.5	1 050	6.2	9 404	23.7
5	75	0.4	225	0.5	1	0.8	15	0.0	74	0.4	225	0.6
6	1	0.0	101	0.2	1	0.8	101	2.0	0	0.0	0	0.0
7	2	0.0	1	0.0	0	0.0	0	0.0	2	0.0	1	0.0
10	4 635	27.1	12 789	28.6	51	43.2	2 394	47.3	4 584	27.0	10 395	26.2
15	8 992	52.7	10 275	23.0	2	1.7	1	0.0	8 990	53.0	10 273	25.9
20	2 297	13.5	10 773	24.1	45	38.1	1 477	29.2	2 252	13.3	9 296	23.4
25	3	0.0	65	0.1	0	0.0	0	0.0	3	0.0	65	0.2
Sub-total	**17 073**	**100.0**	**44 729**	**100.0**	**118**	**100.0**	**5 065**	**100.0**	**16 955.0**	**100.0**	**39 663**	**100.0**
% of all imports	100.0		100.0		0.7		11.3		99.3		88.7	

./...

133

Table 17. (Cont'd) Mexico's MFN import regime as of 31 December 1994
(Import figures in millions of US$)

Tariff	All imports				Subject to import licenses				Not subject to import licenses			
	Number of tariff lines	%	Value of imports	%	Number of tariff lines	%	Value of imports	%	Number of tariff lines	%	Value of imports	%
Agricultural products												
36	1	1.7	9	0.0	0	0.0	0	0.0	1	1.7	0	0.0
45	16	26.7	83	7.0	1	100.0	.6	100.0	15	25.4	82	6.9
46	1	1.7	11	0.9	0	0.0	0	0.0	1	1.7	11	0.9
67	4	6.7	190	15.9	0	0.0	0	0.0	4	6.8	190	16.0
72	4	6.7	2	0.2	0	0.0	0	0.0	4	6.8	2	0.2
118	2	3.3	6	0.5	0	0.0	0	0.0	2	3.4	6	0.6
123	2	3.3	1	0.1	0	0.0	0	0.0	2	3.4	1	0.1
125	6	10.0	13	1.2	0	0.0	0	0.0	6	10.2	13	1.2
128	3	5.0	374	31.3	0	0.0	0.0	0	3	5.1	374	31.4
141	2	3.3	6	0.5	0	0.0	0	0.0	2	3.4	6	0.5
161	2	3.3	23	2.0	0	0.0	0	0.0	2	3.4	23	2.0
198	1	1.7	256	21.5	0	0.0	0	0.0	1	1.7	256	21.5
240	11	18.3	191	16.0	0	0.0	0	0.0	11	18.6	191	16.0
251	1	1.7	7	0.6	0	0.0	0	0.0	1	1.7	7	0.6
260	4	6.7	24	2.1	0	0.0	0	0.0	4	6.8	24	2.1
Sub-total	60	100.0	1 194	100.0	1	100.0	.6	100.0	59	100.0	1 193	100.0
% of all imports	100		100		1.7		0		98.3		100	
Grand total	17 133		45 923		119		5 066		17 014		40 856	
% of all imports	100		100		0.7		11		99.3		89	

Note: Due to the rounding-off of figures, totals might not equal the sum of their components.

Source: SECOFI

Table 18. Tariff summary data for non-agricultural products, December 1994

	All imports	Imports subject to licenses	Imports not subject to licenses
Simple average	12.5	12.1	12.8
Dispersion	6.0	4.8	6.0
Weighted average	11.3	10.9	11.4
Weighted dispersion	8.1	7.0	8.2

Source: SECOFI

Table 19. Evolution of the parastatal sector in Mexico, 1982-May 1993

Type of firm	1982	1983	1984	1985	1986	1987	1988	1989	1990	1991	1992	1993
Decentralised organisms	102	97	95	96	94	94	89	88	82	78	82	82
Majority government participation	744	700	703	629	528	437	252	229	147	120	100	99
Public trusts	231	199	173	147	108	83	71	62	51	43	35	32
Minority government participation	78	78	78	69	7	3	0	0	0	0	0	0
Total	**1 155**	**1 074**	**1 049**	**941**	**737**	**617**	**412**	**379**	**280**	**241**	**217**	**213**

Source: Jacques Rogozinski, La Privatizacion de empresas paraestatales Fondo de Cultura Economica, Mexico D.F., p. 47

Table 20. Types of non-tariff measures imposed by individual Latin American countries against the world (1991)

Country	Total imports 1988 US$ millions	Trade covered by non-tariff measures (%)						
		Total	Para-tariff	AD/CV	Variable levies	Non-automatic licenses	Quotas prohibition	State Monopolies
Argentina	4 122.5	0.3	0	0.1	0	0.2	0	0
Brazil	20 859.9	20.9	0.5	0	0	20.4	0	20.2
Chile	7 285.0	1.9	0	0.2	1.7	0	0	0
Colombia	6 367.7	1.6	0	0	0	1.6	0	0
Mexico	22 767.6	12.9	0	1.4	0	8.6	1.0	6.2
Venezuela	8 845.3	0	0	0	0	0	0	0
Total	**70 248.3**	**10.8**	**0.2**	**0.5**	**0.2**	**9.0**	**0.3**	**8.0**

Notes: In the "Total" row, the percentage of trade covered by different types of NTMs is a trade weighted average of the percentages for the individual countries.

Due to the rounding-off of figures, totals might not equal the sum of their components.

Source: Sam Laird (1995), "Latin American Trade Liberalisation", *Minnesota Journal of Global Trade*, vol 4, issue 2

Table 21. Developed country reductions in bound tariff rates by major industrial product groups

(US$ Billions and percentages)

| Product category | Import value | | Tariff averages weighted by: | | | | | |
| | All sources | Developing economies | Imports from all sources | | | Imports from developing economies | | |
			Pre-UR	Post-UR	% Red.	Pre-UR	Post-UR	% Red.
Industrial products	736.9	169.7	6.3	3.8	40	6.8	4.3	37
Fish & fish products	18.5	10.6	6.1	4.5	26	6.6	4.8	27
Wood, pulp, paper & furniture	40.6	11.5	3.5	1.1	69	4.6	1.7	63
Textile and clothing	66.4	33.2	15.5	12.1	22	14.6	11.3	23
Leather, rubber, footwear	31.7	12.2	8.9	7.3	18	8.1	6.6	19
Metals	69.4	24.4	3.7	1.4	62	2.7	0.9	67
Chemicals & photographic supplies	61.0	8.2	6.7	3.7	45	7.2	3.8	47
Transport equipment	96.3	7.6	7.5	5.8	23	3.8	3.1	18
Non-electrical machinery	118.1	9.8	4.8	1.9	60	4.7	1.6	66
Electrical machinery	86.0	19.2	6.6	3.5	47	6.3	3.3	48
Mineral products & precious stones	73.0	22.2	2.3	1.1	52	2.6	0.8	69
Manufactured articles (n.e.s.)[1]	76.1	10.9	5.5	2.4	56	6.5	3.1	52

1.   Not elsewhere specified

Source: Richard Blackhurst, Alice Enders and Joseph François (1995), "The Uruguay Round and Market Access: Opportunities and Challenges for Developing Countries", paper presented at the World Bank Conference on The Uruguay Round and the Developing Economies, 26-27 January, Washington D.C.

Table 22. Tariff bindings on industrial and agricultural products
(per cent)

URUGUAY

	Industrial products				Agricultural products			
	Tariff lines bound %		Imports under bound rates %		Tariff lines bound %		Imports under bound rates %	
	Pre-	Post-	Pre-	Post-	Pre-	Post-	Pre-	Post-
Total	**43**	**83**	**68**	**87**	**35**	**100**	**63**	**100**
By major country group:								
Developed countries	78	99	94	99	58	100	81	100
Developing countries	21	73	13	61	17	100	22	100
Transition economies	73	98	74	96	57	100	59	100
By region:								
North America	99	100	99	100	92	100	94	100
Latin America	38	100	57	100	36	100	74	100
Western Europe	79	82	98	98	45	100	87	100
Central Europe	63	98	68	97	49	100	54	100
Africa	13	69	26	90	12	100	8	100
Asia	16	68	32	70	15	100	36	100

Source: GATT (1994), The Results of the Uruguay Round of Multilateral Negotiations, Geneva

Table 23. Import protection, based on applied MFN rates and tariff equivalents of NTBs (merchandise imports, excluding primary and processed agriculture)

Import source	Importing region						
	Developed countries	Africa [i]	East Asia	South Asia	Latin America	Other developing	Transition economies
Pre-Uruguay Round							
All sources	0.07	0.18	0.09	0.46	0.24	0.19	0.1
Developing countries							
Africa [i]	0.03	0.16	0.06	0.35	0.16	0.22	0.04
China	0.15	0.25	0.02	0.49	0.26	0.16	0.11
East Asia	0.12	0.23	0.09	0.51	0.27	0.18	0.12
South Asia	0.25	0.26	0.08	0.52	0.29	0.17	0.13
Latin America	0.07	0.17	0.08	0.55	0.22	0.21	0.1
Other developing	0.08	0.12	0.13	0.59	0.16	0.24	0.05
Transition economies	0.07	0.17	0.11	0.45	0.22	0.17	0.06
Post Uruguay Round							
All sources	0.05	0.18	0.06	0.33	0.18	0.15	0.08
Developing countries							
Africa [i]	0.01	0.16	0.04	0.25	0.12	0.16	0.03
China	0.07	0.25	0.01	0.34	0.19	0.13	0.09
East Asia	0.07	0.23	0.06	0.38	0.2	0.14	0.1
South Asia	0.09	0.26	0.05	0.40	0.21	0.13	0.10
Latin America	0.04	0.17	0.05	0.35	0.17	0.16	0.08
Other developing	0.04	0.12	0.09	0.54	0.12	0.18	0.04
Transition economies	0.05	0.17	0.07	0.30	0.16	0.13	0.05

.../...

Table 23 (Cont'd). Import protection, based on applied MFN rates and tariff equivalents of NTBs (merchandise imports, excluding primary and processed agriculture)

Import source	Importing region						
	Developed countries	Africa [1]	East Asia	South Asia	Latin America	Other developing	Transition economies
Relative change							
All sources	-0.29	0.0	-0.27	-0.3	-0.27	-0.23	-0.18
Developing countries							
Africa [2]	-0.43	0.0	-0.3	-0.3	-0.23	-0.26	-0.18
China	-0.51	0.0	-0.3	-0.3	-0.26	-0.22	-0.2
East Asia	-0.47	0.0	-0.29	-0.26	-0.27	-0.23	-0.17
South Asia	-0.65	0.0	-0.31	-0.22	-0.27	-0.23	-0.21
Latin America	-0.45	0.0	-0.35	-0.36	-0.26	-0.26	-0.18
Other developing	-0.5	0.0	-0.28	-0.08	-0.22	-0.23	-0.2
Transition economies	-0.37	0.0	-0.41	-0.34	-0.26	-0.25	-0.17

1. Excludes South Africa
2. Import weights exclude South Africa and include Middle East. Tariffs of the latter are not included in the integrated data base.

Source: Richard Blackhurst, Alice Enders and Joseph François (1995), "The Uruguay Round and Market Access: Opportunities and Challenges for Developing Countries", paper presented at the World Bank Conference on The Uruguay Round and the Developing Economies, 26-27 January, Washington D.C.

Table 24. Mexico: applied and bound MFN tariff rates

Product category	Value of imports[1] (000US$)	Number of lines	Import[1] weighted average MFN rates			% of imports[1] for which post-UR bound rates ≥pre-UR applied rates
			Pre-UR applied rates	Pre-UR bound rates	Post-UR bound rates	
Agriculture[2], excluding fish	2 895 830	1 030	4.98	76.9	67.01	98.3
Fish and fish products	41 477	126	11.73	48.85	34.93	100.0
Wood, pulp, paper and furniture	751 922	498	5.54	33.22	25.14	100.0
Textiles and clothing	335 213	1 127	15.62	49.62	34.90	100.0
Leather, rubber, footwear	301 140	269	11.60	48.85	34.71	100.0
Metals	1 128 064	1 319	9.48	45.44	32.88	100.0
Chemicals and photographic supplies	2 009 052	2 561	7.74	46.42	33.86	100.0
Transport equipment	1 023 513	349	14.74	48.28	36.69	100.0
Non-electrical machinery	2 818 969	1 672	11.94	47.57	35.08	100.0
Electrical machinery	1 466 868	1 013	14.46	48.07	34.77	100.0
Minerals products, precious stones and metals	564 784	624	9.02	39.06	28.39	100.0
Manufactured articles (n.e.s.)[3]	804 990	1 023	13.90	46.55	34.01	96.3
Crude petroleum oils	340 558	22	8.40	50.00	35.00	100.0
All merchandise trade	14 462 380	12 308	9.88	52.22	40.36	99.4

1. World imports 1988.
2. The pre-Uruguay Round rate is the MFN base rate; the post-Uruguay Round rate includes the results of tariffication of non-tariff barriers.
3. Not elsewhere specified.
Source: WTO Integrated Data Base

LIST OF CHARTS

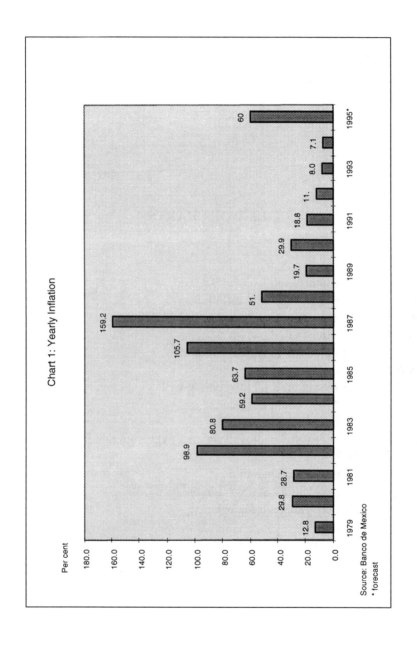

Chart 1: Yearly Inflation

Per cent

Source: Banco de Mexico
* forecast

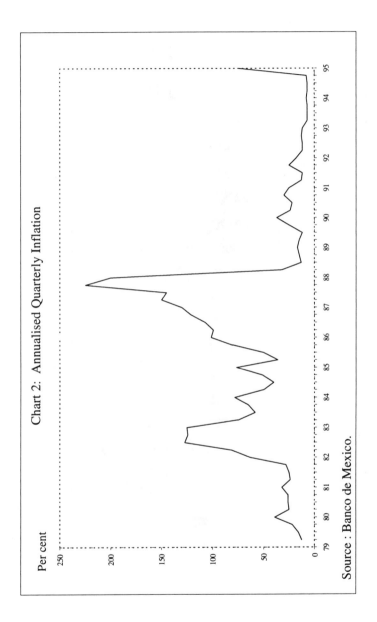

Chart 2: Annualised Quarterly Inflation

Source : Banco de Mexico.

145

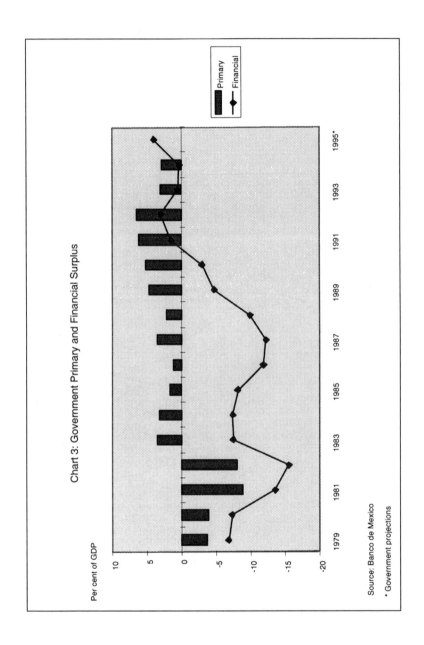

Chart 3: Government Primary and Financial Surplus

Per cent of GDP

Source: Banco de Mexico

* Government projections

146

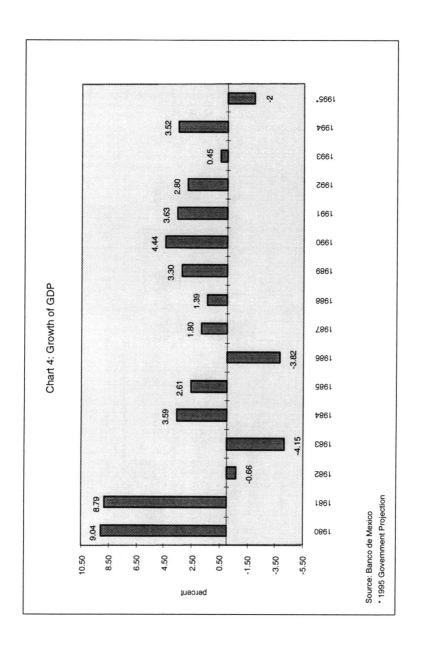

Chart 4: Growth of GDP

Year	percent
1980	9.04
1981	8.79
1982	-0.66
1983	-4.15
1984	3.59
1985	2.61
1986	-3.82
1987	1.80
1988	1.39
1989	3.30
1990	4.44
1991	3.63
1992	2.80
1993	0.45
1994	3.52
1995*	-2

Source: Banco de Mexico
* 1995 Government Projection

147

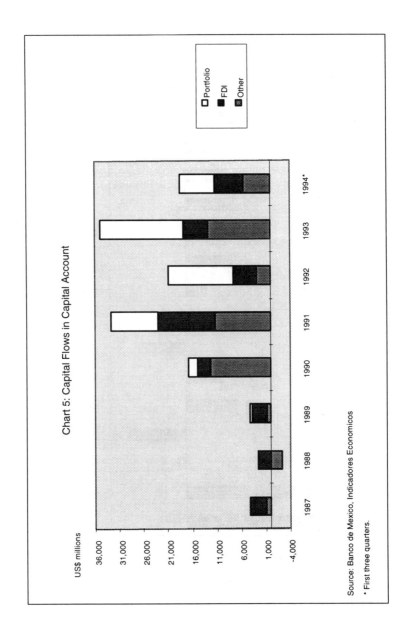

Chart 5: Capital Flows in Capital Account

US$ millions

Source: Banco de Mexico, Indicadores Economicos

* First three quarters.

148

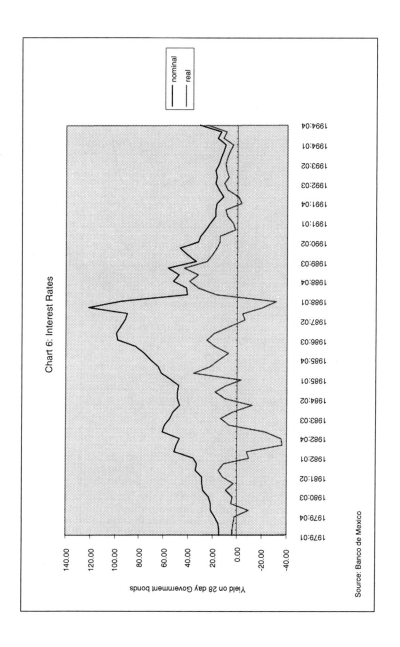

Chart 6: Interest Rates

Yield on 28 day Government bonds

Source: Banco de Mexico

149

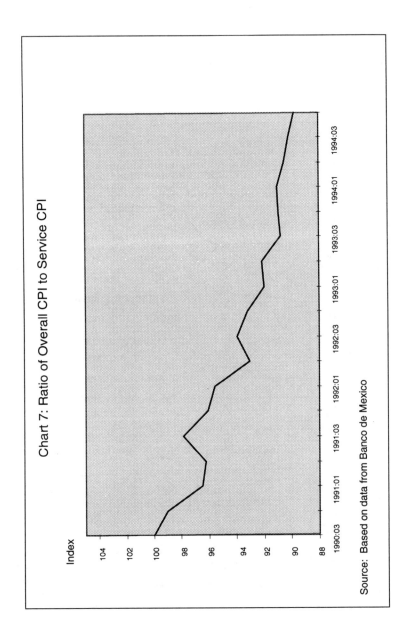

Chart 7: Ratio of Overall CPI to Service CPI

Source: Based on data from Banco de Mexico

150

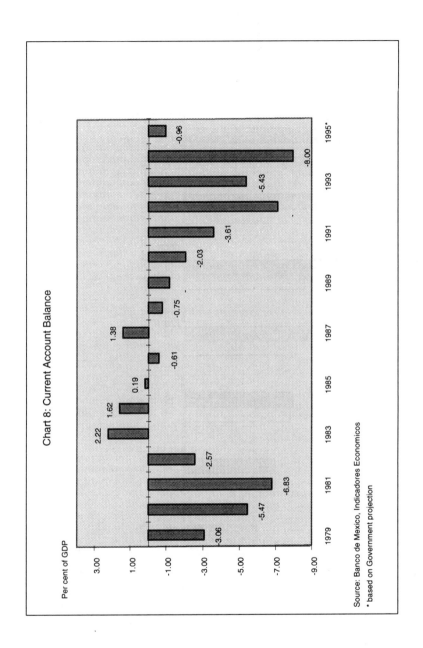

Chart 8: Current Account Balance

Per cent of GDP

Source: Banco de Mexico, Indicadores Economicos
* based on Government projection

151

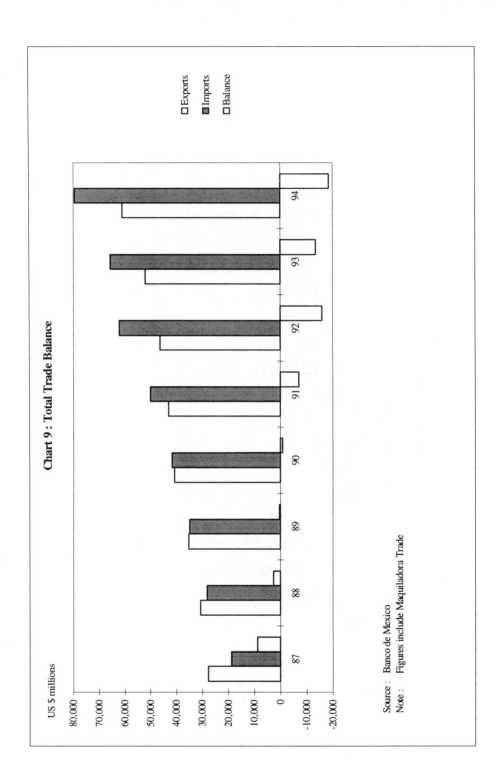

Chart 9 : Total Trade Balance

US $ millions

Source :   Banco de Mexico
Note :   Figures include Maquiladora Trade

152

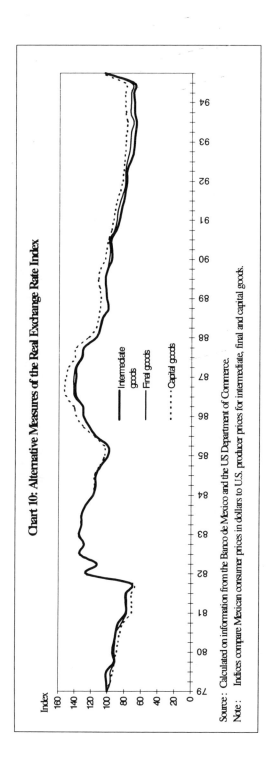

Chart 10: Alternative Measures of the Real Exchange Rate Index

Source : Calculated on information from the Banco de Mexico and the US Department of Commerce.

Note : Indices compare Mexican consumer prices in dollars to U.S. producer prices for intermediate, final and capital goods.

153

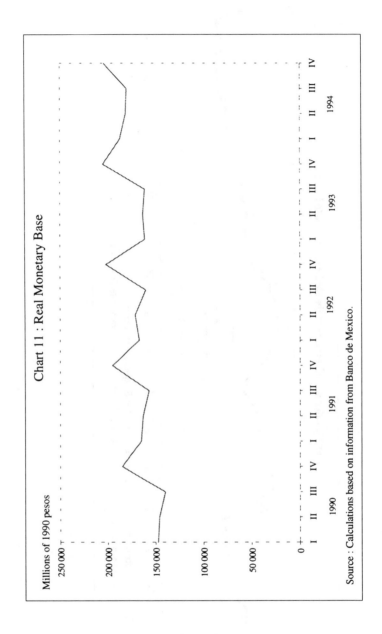

Chart 11 : Real Monetary Base

Source : Calculations based on information from Banco de Mexico.

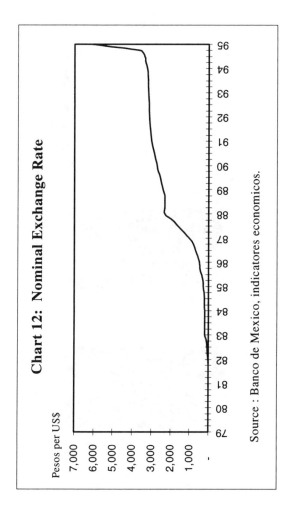

Chart 12: Nominal Exchange Rate

Pesos per US$

Source : Banco de Mexico, indicatores economicos.

155

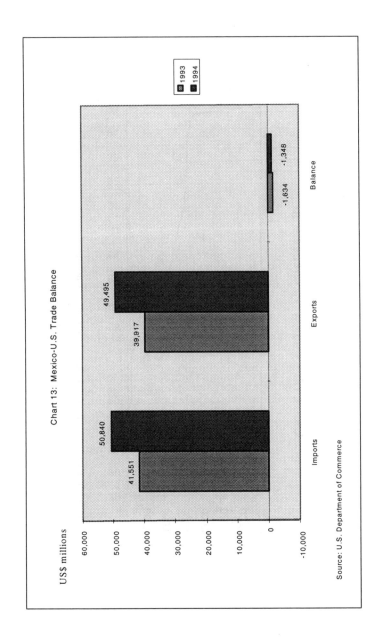

Chart 13: Mexico-U.S. Trade Balance

US$ millions

Source: U.S. Department of Commerce

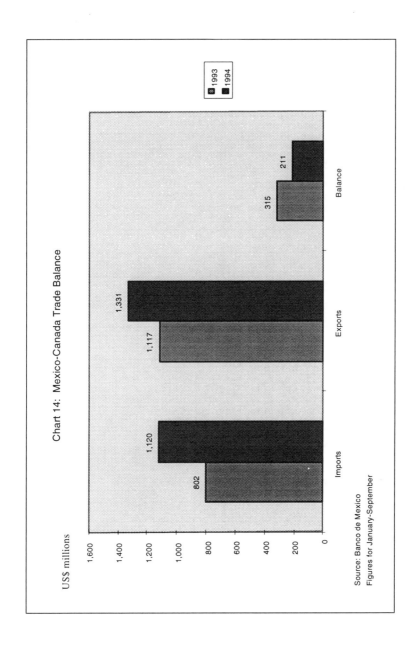

Chart 14: Mexico-Canada Trade Balance

US$ millions

1,600
1,400
1,200
1,000
800
600
400
200
0

Imports   Exports   Balance

802
1,120
1,117
1,331
315
211

1993
1994

Source: Banco de Mexico
Figures for January-September

MAIN SALES OUTLETS OF OECD PUBLICATIONS
PRINCIPAUX POINTS DE VENTE DES PUBLICATIONS DE L'OCDE

AUSTRALIA – AUSTRALIE
D.A. Information Services
648 Whitehorse Road, P.O.B 163
Mitcham, Victoria 3132   Tel. (03) 9210.7777
Fax: (03) 9210.7788

AUSTRIA – AUTRICHE
Gerold & Co.
Graben 31
Wien I   Tel. (0222) 533.50.14
Fax: (0222) 512.47.31.29

BELGIUM – BELGIQUE
Jean De Lannoy
Avenue du Roi, Koningslaan 202
B-1060 Bruxelles
Tel. (02) 538.51.69/538.08.41
Fax: (02) 538.08.41

CANADA
Renouf Publishing Company Ltd.
1294 Algoma Road
Ottawa, ON K1B 3W8   Tel. (613) 741.4333
Fax: (613) 741.5439

Stores:
61 Sparks Street
Ottawa, ON K1P 5R1   Tel. (613) 238.8985

12 Adelaide Street West
Toronto, ON M5H 1L6   Tel. (416) 363.3171
Fax: (416)363.59.63

Les Éditions La Liberté Inc.
3020 Chemin Sainte-Foy
Sainte-Foy, PQ G1X 3V6 Tel. (418) 658.3763
Fax: (418) 658.3763

Federal Publications Inc.
165 University Avenue, Suite 701
Toronto, ON M5H 3B8   Tel. (416) 860.1611
Fax: (416) 860.1608

Les Publications Fédérales
1185 Université
Montréal, QC H3B 3A7   Tel. (514) 954.1633
Fax: (514) 954.1635

CHINA – CHINE
China National Publications Import
Export Corporation (CNPIEC)
16 Gongti E. Road, Chaoyang District
P.O. Box 88 or 50
Beijing 100704 PR   Tel. (01) 506.6688
Fax: (01) 506.3101

CHINESE TAIPEI – TAIPEI CHINOIS
Good Faith Worldwide Int'l. Co. Ltd.
9th Floor, No. 118, Sec. 2
Chung Hsiao E. Road
Taipei   Tel. (02) 391.7396/391.7397
Fax: (02) 394.9176

**CZECH REPUBLIC – RÉPUBLIQUE
TCHÈQUE**
National Information Centre
NIS – prodejna
Konviktská 5
Praha 1 – 113 57   Tel. (02) 24.23.09.07
Fax: (02) 24.22.94.33
(*Contact* Ms Jana Pospisilova,
nkposp@dec.niz.cz)

DENMARK – DANEMARK
Munksgaard Book and Subscription Service
35, Nørre Søgade, P.O. Box 2148
DK-1016 København K   Tel. (33) 12.85.70
Fax: (33) 12.93.87

J. H. Schultz Information A/S,
Herstedvang 12,
DK – 2620 Albertslung   Tel. 43 63 23 00
Fax: 43 63 19 69
Internet: s-info@inet.uni-c.dk

EGYPT – ÉGYPTE
The Middle East Observer
41 Sherif Street
Cairo   Tel. 392.6919
Fax: 360-6804

FINLAND – FINLANDE
Akateeminen Kirjakauppa
Keskuskatu 1, P.O. Box 128
00100 Helsinki

Subscription Services/Agence d'abonnements :
P.O. Box 23
00371 Helsinki   Tel. (358 0) 121 4416
Fax: (358 0) 121.4450

FRANCE
OECD/OCDE
Mail Orders/Commandes par correspondance :
2, rue André-Pascal
75775 Paris Cedex 16 Tel. (33-1) 45.24.82.00
Fax: (33-1) 49.10.42.76
Telex: 640048 OCDE
Internet: Compte.PUBSINQ@oecd.org

Orders via Minitel, France only/
Commandes par Minitel, France exclusive-
ment :
36 15 OCDE

OECD Bookshop/Librairie de l'OCDE :
33, rue Octave-Feuillet
75016 Paris   Tél. (33-1) 45.24.81.81
(33-1) 45.24.81.67

Dawson
B.P. 40
91121 Palaiseau Cedex   Tel. 69.10.47.00
Fax: 64.54.83.26

Documentation Française
29, quai Voltaire
75007 Paris   Tel. 40.15.70.00

Economica
49, rue Héricart
75015 Paris   Tel. 45.75.05.67
Fax: 40.58.15.70

Gibert Jeune (Droit-Économie)
6, place Saint-Michel
75006 Paris   Tel. 43.25.91.19

Librairie du Commerce International
10, avenue d'Iéna
75016 Paris   Tel. 40.73.34.60

Librairie Dunod
Université Paris-Dauphine
Place du Maréchal-de-Lattre-de-Tassigny
75016 Paris   Tel. 44.05.40.13

Librairie Lavoisier
11, rue Lavoisier
75008 Paris   Tel. 42.65.39.95

Librairie des Sciences Politiques
30, rue Saint-Guillaume
75007 Paris   Tel. 45.48.36.02

P.U.F.
49, boulevard Saint-Michel
75005 Paris   Tel. 43.25.83.40

Librairie de l'Université
12a, rue Nazareth
13100 Aix-en-Provence Tel. (16) 42.26.18.08

Documentation Française
165, rue Garibaldi
69003 Lyon   Tel. (16) 78.63.32.23

Librairie Decitre
29, place Bellecour
69002 Lyon   Tel. (16) 72.40.54.54

Librairie Sauramps
Le Triangle
34967 Montpellier Cedex 2
Tel. (16) 67.58.85.15
Fax: (16) 67.58.27.36

A la Sorbonne Actual
23, rue de l'Hôtel-des-Postes
06000 Nice   Tel. (16) 93.13.77.75
Fax: (16) 93.80.75.69

GERMANY – ALLEMAGNE
OECD Bonn Centre
August-Bebel-Allee 6
D-53175 Bonn   Tel. (0228) 959.120
Fax: (0228) 959.12.17

GREECE – GRÈCE
Librairie Kauffmann
Stadiou 28
10564 Athens   Tel. (01) 32.55.321
Fax: (01) 32.30.320

HONG-KONG
Swindon Book Co. Ltd.
Astoria Bldg. 3F
34 Ashley Road, Tsimshatsui
Kowloon, Hong Kong   Tel. 2376.2062
Fax: 2376.0685

HUNGARY – HONGRIE
Euro Info Service
Margitsziget, Európa Ház
1138 Budapest   Tel. (1) 111.62.16
Fax: (1) 111.60.61

ICELAND – ISLANDE
Mál Mog Menning
Laugavegi 18, Pósthólf 392
121 Reykjavik   Tel. (1) 552.4240
Fax: (1) 562.3523

INDIA – INDE
Oxford Book and Stationery Co.
Scindia House
New Delhi 110001   Tel. (11) 331.5896/5308
Fax: (11) 371.8275

17 Park Street
Calcutta 700016   Tel. 240832

INDONESIA – INDONÉSIE
Pdii-Lipi
P.O. Box 4298
Jakarta 12042   Tel. (21) 573.34.67
Fax: (21) 573.34.67

IRELAND – IRLANDE
Government Supplies Agency
Publications Section
4/5 Harcourt Road
Dublin 2   Tel. 661.31.11
Fax: 475.27.60

ISRAEL – ISRAËL
Praedicta
5 Shatner Street
P.O. Box 34030
Jerusalem 91430   Tel. (2) 52.84.90/1/2
Fax: (2) 52.84.93

R.O.Y. International
P.O. Box 13056
Tel Aviv 61130   Tel. (3) 546 1423
Fax: (3) 546 1442

Palestinian Authority/Middle East:
INDEX Information Services
P.O.B. 19502
Jerusalem   Tel. (2) 27.12.19
Fax: (2) 27.16.34

ITALY – ITALIE
Libreria Commissionaria Sansoni
Via Duca di Calabria 1/1
50125 Firenze   Tel. (055) 64.54.15
Fax: (055) 64.12.57

Via Bartolini 29
20155 Milano   Tel. (02) 36.50.83

Editrice e Libreria Herder
Piazza Montecitorio 120
00186 Roma   Tel. 679.46.28
Fax: 678.47.51

Libreria Hoepli
Via Hoepli 5
20121 Milano   Tel. (02) 86.54.46
                             Fax: (02) 805.28.86
Libreria Scientifica
Dott. Lucio de Biasio 'Aeiou'
Via Coronelli, 6
20146 Milano   Tel. (02) 48.95.45.52
                             Fax: (02) 48.95.45.48

JAPAN - JAPON
OECD Tokyo Centre
Landic Akasaka Building
2-3-4 Akasaka, Minato-ku
Tokyo 107   Tel. (81.3) 3586.2016
                             Fax: (81.3) 3584.7929

KOREA - CORÉE
Kyobo Book Centre Co. Ltd.
P.O. Box 1658, Kwang Hwa Moon
Seoul   Tel. 730.78.91
                             Fax: 735.00.30

MALAYSIA - MALAISIE
University of Malaya Bookshop
University of Malaya
P.O. Box 1127, Jalan Pantai Baru
59700 Kuala Lumpur
Malaysia   Tel. 756.5000/756.5425
                             Fax: 756.3246

MEXICO - MEXIQUE
OECD Mexico Centre
Edificio INFOTEC
Av. San Fernando no. 37
Col. Toriello Guerra
Tlalpan C.P. 14050
Mexico D.F.   Tel. (525) 665 47 99
                             Fax: (525) 606 13 07

NETHERLANDS - PAYS-BAS
SDU Uitgeverij Plantijnstraat
Externe Fondsen
Postbus 20014
2500 EA's-Gravenhage   Tel. (070) 37.89.880
Voor bestellingen: Fax: (070) 34.75.778

Subscription Agency/Agence d'abonnements :
SWETS & ZEITLINGER BV
Heereweg 347B
P.O. Box 830
2160 SZ Lisse   Tel. 252.435.111
                             Fax: 252.415.888

NEW ZEALAND -
NOUVELLE-ZÉLANDE
GPLegislation Services
P.O. Box 12418
Thorndon, Wellington   Tel. (04) 496.5655
                             Fax: (04) 496.5698

NORWAY - NORVÈGE
NIC INFO A/S
Ostensjoveien 18
P.O. Box 6512 Etterstad
0606 Oslo   Tel. (22) 97.45.00
                             Fax: (22) 97.45.45

PAKISTAN
Mirza Book Agency
65 Shahrah Quaid-E-Azam
Lahore 54000   Tel. (42) 735.36.01
                             Fax: (42) 576.37.14

PHILIPPINE - PHILIPPINES
International Booksource Center Inc.
Rm 179/920 Cityland 10 Condo Tower 2
HV dela Costa Ext cor Valero St.
Makati Metro Manila   Tel. (632) 817 9676
                       Fax: (632) 817 1741

POLAND - POLOGNE
Ars Polona
00-950 Warszawa
Krakowskie Prezdmiescie 7 Tel. (22) 264760
                           Fax: (22) 265334

PORTUGAL
Livraria Portugal
Rua do Carmo 70-74
Apart. 2681
1200 Lisboa   Tel. (01) 347.49.82/5
                           Fax: (01) 347.02.64

SINGAPORE - SINGAPOUR
Ashgate Publishing
Asia Pacific Pte. Ltd
Golden Wheel Building, 04-03
41, Kallang Pudding Road
Singapore 349316   Tel. 741.5166
                           Fax: 742.9356

SPAIN - ESPAGNE
Mundi-Prensa Libros S.A.
Castelló 37, Apartado 1223
Madrid 28001   Tel. (91) 431.33.99
                           Fax: (91) 575.39.98

Mundi-Prensa Barcelona
Consell de Cent No. 391
08009 - Barcelona   Tel. (93) 488.34.92
                           Fax: (93) 487.76.59

Llibreria de la Generalitat
Palau Moja
Rambla dels Estudis, 118
08002 - Barcelona
              (Subscripcions) Tel. (93) 318.80.12
              (Publicacions) Tel. (93) 302.67.23
                           Fax: (93) 412.18.54

SRI LANKA
Centre for Policy Research
c/o Colombo Agencies Ltd.
No. 300-304, Galle Road
Colombo 3   Tel. (1) 574240, 573551-2
                  Fax: (1) 575394, 510711

SWEDEN - SUÈDE
CE Fritzes AB
S-106 47 Stockholm   Tel. (08) 690.90.90
                           Fax: (08) 20.50.21

For electronic publications only/
Publications électroniques seulement
STATISTICS SWEDEN
Informationsservice
S-115 81 Stockholm   Tel. 8 783 5066
                           Fax: 8 783 4045

Subscription Agency/Agence d'abonnements :
Wennergren-Williams Info AB
P.O. Box 1305
171 25 Solna   Tel. (08) 705.97.50
                           Fax: (08) 27.00.71

SWITZERLAND - SUISSE
Maditec S.A. (Books and Periodicals/Livres
et périodiques)
Chemin des Palettes 4
Case postale 266
1020 Renens VD 1   Tel. (021) 635.08.65
                           Fax: (021) 635.07.80

Librairie Payot S.A.
4, place Pépinet
CP 3212
1002 Lausanne   Tel. (021) 320.25.11
                           Fax: (021) 320.25.14

Librairie Unilivres
6, rue de Candolle
1205 Genève   Tel. (022) 320.26.23
                           Fax: (022) 329.73.18

Subscription Agency/Agence d'abonnements :
Dynapresse Marketing S.A.
38, avenue Vibert
1227 Carouge   Tel. (022) 308.08.70
                           Fax: (022) 308.07.99

See also - Voir aussi :
OECD Bonn Centre
August-Bebel-Allee 6
D-53175 Bonn (Germany)
                           Tel. (0228) 959.120
                           Fax: (0228) 959.12.17

THAILAND - THAÏLANDE
Suksit Siam Co. Ltd.
113, 115 Fuang Nakhon Rd.
Opp. Wat Rajbopith
Bangkok 10200   Tel. (662) 225.9531/2
                           Fax: (662) 222.5188

TRINIDAD & TOBAGO, CARIBBEAN
TRINITÉ-ET-TOBAGO, CARAÏBES
SSL Systematics Studies Limited
9 Watts Street
Curepe, Trinadad & Tobago, W.I.
                           Tel. (1809) 645.3475
                           Fax: (1809) 662.5654

TUNISIA - TUNISIE
Grande Librairie Spécialisée
Fendri Ali
Avenue Haffouz Imm El-Intilaka
Bloc B 1 Sfax 3000   Tel. (216-4) 296 855
                      Fax: (216-4) 298.270

TURKEY - TURQUIE
Kültür Yayinlari Is-Türk Ltd. Sti.
Atatürk Bulvari No. 191/Kat 13
06684 Kavaklidere/Ankara
                    Tél. (312) 428.11.40 Ext. 2458
                    Fax : (312) 417.24.90
                    et 425.07.50-51-52-53
Dolmabahce Cad. No. 29
Besiktas/Istanbul   Tel. (212) 260 7188

UNITED KINGDOM - ROYAUME-UNI
HMSO
Gen. enquiries   Tel. (0171) 873 0011
                           Fax: (0171) 873 8463
Postal orders only:
P.O. Box 276, London SW8 5DT
Personal Callers HMSO Bookshop
49 High Holborn, London WC1V 6HB
Branches at: Belfast, Birmingham, Bristol,
Edinburgh, Manchester

UNITED STATES - ÉTATS-UNIS
OECD Washington Center
2001 L Street N.W., Suite 650
Washington, D.C. 20036-4922
                           Tel. (202) 785.6323
                           Fax: (202) 785.0350
Internet: washcont@oecd.org
Subscriptions to OECD periodicals may also
be placed through main subscription agencies.

Les abonnements aux publications périodiques
de l'OCDE peuvent être souscrits auprès des
principales agences d'abonnement.

Orders and inquiries from countries where Distributors have not yet been appointed should be
sent to: OECD Publications, 2, rue André-Pascal, 75775 Paris Cedex 16, France.

Les commandes provenant de pays où l'OCDE
n'a pas encore désigné de distributeur peuvent
être adressées aux Éditions de l'OCDE, 2, rue
André-Pascal, 75775 Paris Cedex 16, France.

8-1996

OECD PUBLICATIONS, 2, rue André-Pascal, 75775 PARIS CEDEX 16
PRINTED IN FRANCE
(22 96 05 1) ISBN 92-64-15316-0 – No. 49089 1996